T0408704

ANNA SPIRO

A LIFE IN PATTERN

ANNA SPIRO

A LIFE IN PATTERN

BY

ANNA SPIRO

PHOTOGRAPHY BY

TIM SALISBURY

DESIGN BY

PENNY SHEEHAN

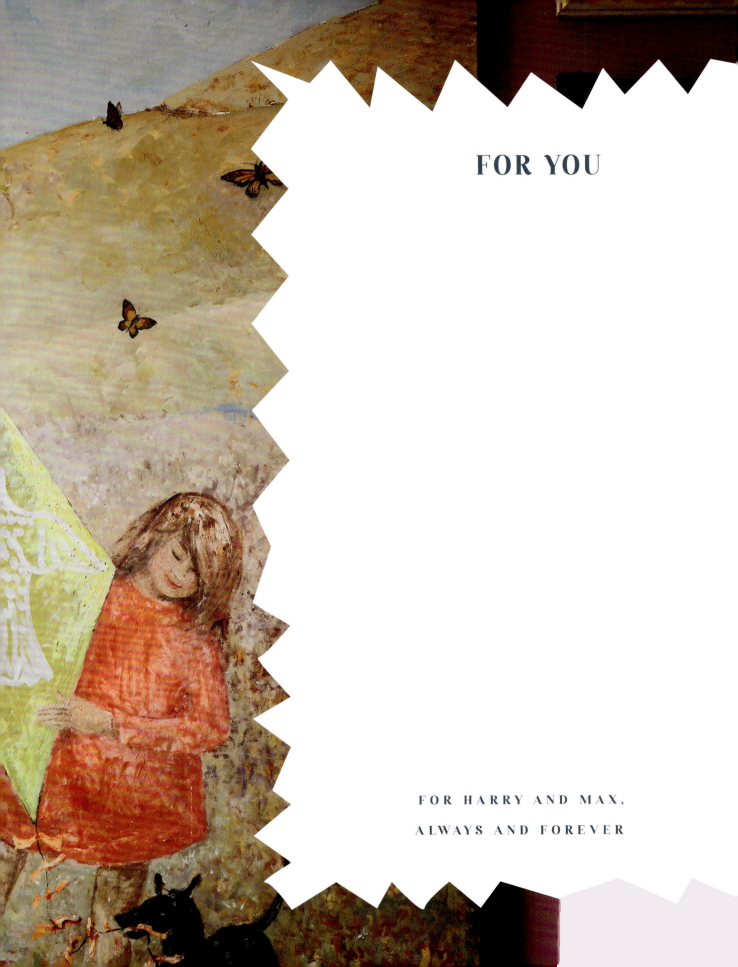

FOR YOU

FOR HARRY AND MAX,
ALWAYS AND FOREVER

SEASONS

As I sit down to pen these first words, I find myself in a very different place from the one I was in when I wrote my first book, *Absolutely Beautiful Things*, eight years ago. My professional and personal lives have completely transformed, backflipped and somersaulted, allowing me to discover a new perspective. Since my early days running a retail shop in Brisbane and undertaking small-scale decorating commissions for clients, my business has grown to take on much larger projects, in both the residential and commercial sectors. I now work with clients across Australia and my business has expanded to include an office in Melbourne.

I am excited that my style and creativity is appreciated by others and consider myself lucky to be constantly presented with so many different creative opportunities. These experiences have shaped my life. I always challenge myself to try new things – I like to play on the expected and go against the tide – all the while pushing myself to perfect my craft. It has always been my deep-seated aspiration to create places that are well-informed and uniquely fabulous, full of soulful qualities, unexpected twists – and most often with traditional groundwork updated to function well in our modern world. The benefits of time and constant practice have allowed me to develop and gain confidence in my work, and consequently to deliver projects that are carefully curated and executed to the nth degree in terms of detail, creativity and quality.

Perhaps one of the most significant projects I have undertaken during this past decade is the transformation of Halcyon House, a twenty-one suite boutique beachfront hotel in northern New South Wales. Designing and decorating Halcyon taught me how to work on a large scale and gave me essential experience in the commercial sector. More than that, however, Halcyon put my work, my style and my distinctive approach to designing interiors for a boutique hotel – the first of its kind in Australia – on the world stage. The project opened many doors for me, and I am forever grateful for the opportunity. My clients took a huge leap of faith in choosing me to create something totally individual for them and their patrons.

After Halcyon, enquiries for new projects came in thick and fast. It was around this time that I started Anna Spiro Textiles with my brother, Sam. It had been a life-long dream to create my own textiles. Colourful, patterned fabrics are always at the centre of my design work and it felt like a natural progression to create my own line. For five years now, we have been producing – from scratch – a range of artisanal fabrics designed and printed in Australia, which we sell worldwide. I must admit, I often have little 'pinch me' moments when I see our fabrics being used in beautiful rooms by talented designers across the world.

While it might seem strange to some, I am propelled and exhilarated by the momentum of being run off my feet. I enjoy the thrill of being busy. However, managing two businesses, along with a retail storefront, became extremely hectic and eventually I had to think about what I really wanted to concentrate on. Although the retail side was fun – and it was always so lovely seeing our regular customers – the decision to close the store was probably one of the best I have made, allowing me to move on to the next stage in my career. The design and decorating, and textiles businesses could now take centre stage.

So after nearly twenty years, I closed the Black & Spiro store, and moved my design and textile businesses a few hundred metres up the road into a gorgeous old Art Deco building. My design business is currently downstairs, but I am in the process of creating a display apartment upstairs by joining three one-bedroom apartments into one large apartment. Eventually it will be a space where I can work, as well as hold client meetings, workshops and events. I wanted to maintain a little street presence, too, so I installed a window display box that the team and I have fun redecorating a few times a year. I like to think it keeps people interested and provides some inspiration – it is almost like a little jewel box on New Farm's busy Brunswick Street.

In 2020, with change in the air, we made the decision as a family to sell Birkdale House, the magnificent 19th-century wooden house where we had lived for a decade; the house I had thought we would live in forever. My present life, with my new partner, sees me spending half my time in Melbourne and the other half in Brisbane, so it just wasn't practical to keep such a large property any longer.

It's important to accept that things change, and we must change with them. Nevertheless, selling the house was one of the hardest things I've done, as it really was a part of me - I had decorated and redecorated, and had a lot of fun experimenting with many different paint colours, fabrics and combinations of furniture and art. I have always loved old buildings - structures created in the times of slow building methods, using talented craftspeople - but selling Birkdale brought the emotional aspects of a home's history into sharp focus. These heritage houses hold the stories of all the people who have lived within their walls. I am part of the history of Birkdale House now, and I will cherish the memories of living there for the rest of my life.

Leaving Birkdale cleared the way for me to embark on an exciting new personal project in Melbourne with my partner, Luke: renovating an 1880s Victorian house that had been left derelict and uninhabited for twenty years. With its grandiose 14-foot (4.3-metre) ceilings, bluestone foundations and untouched characterful features, it is a project I am deeply passionate about. I cannot wait to breathe new life into this lovely old house.

As I reflect on the past decade of my career, I realise that I have, quite simply, grown up. My basic design and decorating principles remain the same, but the ways I can apply them have drastically expanded. In short, I have become better with age and practice. I have learned to roll with the punches, to embrace adaptation. What began as interior decorating has become an almost holistic endeavour; one in which I can now bring to bear all of my skill, knowledge and experience from the very beginning. What I once saw as my practice has become my philosophy.

There can come a time in one's career - if we're lucky - when, suddenly, everything feels like it's coming together as it should. My experiences over the past two decades working in interior design have given me newfound perspective, confidence and energy - both in life and in work. I have entered the next season of my life and it is *exciting*. I have my two beautiful sons, a relationship with a wonderful man, new projects to challenge and stimulate me, and hopefully many more adventures ahead. And so, it felt like the right time to write this book, as a way to share with you my perspective at this rather bright and balanced point in my life - my thoughts, my experiences and some of the lovely projects I have been working on over the past few years.

TRADEMARK
Style

WHAT MAKES A HOME

ONE'S OWN?

This is one of those questions that I come back to time and again. Home should be a place of normality and familiarity, of comfort; a place that wraps you up and makes you feel safe, warm and happy. Home is where you can create your own world – and what makes my home mine is completely different to what makes your home yours.

So, how do we create a place that we truly adore and cherish? The things we love, collect and arrange within our home make it feel like 'us'. Without them, a home can feel empty and soulless. I have been creating a home that I love ever since I left my family home in my early twenties. Yes, I have lived in a number of houses since then, but much of the furniture, art and other bits and pieces that I have collected have stayed with me. These elements have travelled with me on my journey and I have reworked them into my various houses. They are kind of like old friends; a new house feels more like a home the moment I put my old friends inside it.

I have worked with a number of clients who have entered the later stages of their lives – their children have left home and they are at the point of downsizing from a large family home to an apartment or townhouse. One of the most common things I notice when such clients come to me is that they are not ready to let go of their things – objects that they have loved, that have been familiar to them for their entire lives in some cases. Often, a couple's children will push for them to move the old furniture on and start from scratch, but I almost always advise the opposite. For one, I understand that getting rid of those treasured pieces can be like losing an arm or a leg. Moreover, by incorporating some of those special old items into the new home, while mixing in some fresh new pieces, we can create a sense of familiarity that makes transitioning to a brand-new place that bit easier.

THE WORLD OF INTERIORS SEPTEMBER 2018

THE WORLD OF INTERIORS DECEMBER 2012

THE WORLD OF INTERIORS JULY 2018

THE WORLD OF INTERIORS JANUARY 2018

THE WORLD OF INTERIORS SEPTEMBER 2017

THE WORLD OF INTERIORS DECEMBER 2017

THE WORLD OF INTERIORS JULY 2016

THE WORLD OF INTERIORS FEBRUARY 2016

THE WORLD OF INTERIORS JANUARY 2016

THE WORLD OF INTERIORS MAY 2016

THE WORLD OF INTERIORS JUNE 2012

THE WORLD OF INTERIORS AUGUST 2012

THE WORLD OF INTERIORS APRIL 2016

THE WORLD OF INTERIORS DECEMBER 2016

THE WORLD OF INTERIORS 2017

THE WORLD OF INTERIORS

DOLLY

The Kookery & The Wild

Ever since I was a young girl, I would buck at anything my mother told me to wear. I never wanted to dress like all the other girls. I wanted to choose my own clothes and be different. It was my chance to express myself and explore my taste and style. I have always loved to be different, and embraced things that are a bit kooky and aren't necessarily in fashion. My teachers at school used to say I had a wild imagination. I think my 'out-there' creative ideas are my strong point, my advantage, and they form my own unique style.

Even today, my children look at me sideways at times, trying to get a grasp on where I am coming from with my off-beat ideas. Most recently, my son Harry had a lot to say about the many different paint colours and wallpapers I had used in the first stage of my office–apartment renovation.

In both my design work and my fashion choices, I am always searching for special things; things that nobody else wants, things that aren't necessarily cool. My heart skips a beat when I find a particular old piece of furniture or a stunning roll of fabric that I have never seen before. I don't like to rehash the same fabrics over and over. There are so many incredible fabrics in the world, why not use something different each time? I like my designs to be fresh and full of interesting, contradictory elements. Sometimes I do have favourite fabrics, but if I decide to use them again, I always find new, imaginative ways of putting them together.

A lot of people try so hard to make everything match perfectly. To be honest, I am the complete opposite. I actually find it challenging to create a plain, straightforwardly matching scheme – it goes against every single grain in my body. What really excites me is throwing caution to the wind: painting the walls of a formal room in a wild, bright colour, then hanging them with dark old gilt-framed oil paintings; and juxtaposing that with fresh floral chintz-covered sofas placed on a modern geometric-patterned rug. It's these types of offbeat, playful concepts that really delight me. Clients come to me because they are attracted to my signature eclectic style, but I believe each of my clients needs to have their own look, their own individual style – and that's what I try to help them unearth.

LIAN HEARN — *the storyteller and his three daughters*

The GENIUS of BIRDS — JENNIFER ACKERMAN — SCRIBE

A NATURE POEM FOR EVERY DAY OF THE YEAR — BATSFORD

BILL **BRYSON** — THE BODY

GIRT — DAVID HUNT — Black Inc.

TRUE GIRT — DAVID HUNT — Black Inc.

MAO'S LAST DANCER — LI CUNXIN

DR MICHAEL MOSLEY — the clever guts diet

MARGARET & GOUGH — SUSAN MITCHELL

LIFE'S A PITCH — PHILIP DELVES BROUGHTON

MADE BY HUMANS

WE ARE ONE VILLAGE

Dr. David B. Agus

BRAVE

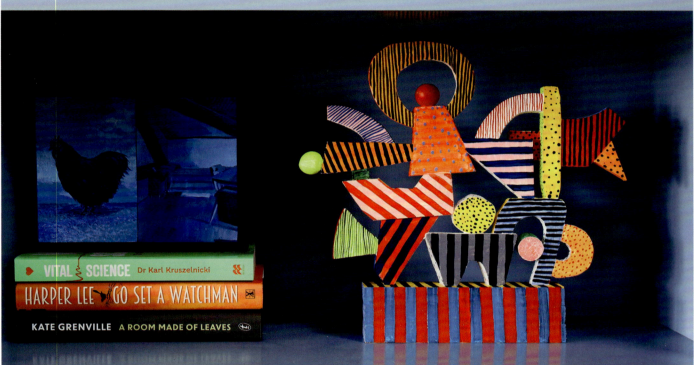

VITAL SCIENCE — Dr Karl Kruszelnicki

HARPER LEE — GO SET A WATCHMAN

KATE GRENVILLE — A ROOM MADE OF LEAVES

SHE IS FIERCE — Ana Sampson

PAUL BANGAY — SMALL GARDEN DESIGN

HEALING HOTELS OF THE WORLD

DR. SUITS — Oh, the MEETINGS You'll Go To! — PORTFOLIO/PENGUIN

Stephanie Alexander — A Shared Table

50 OF THE WORLD'S BEST **APARTMENTS**

MAKING SOMETHING
OUT OF NOTHING

One of the challenges I enjoy the most is creating something out of nothing. I like to make spaces feel exciting yet comfortable, interesting yet harmonious. When presented with a house or room with not much going for it, I think about what I can add to make it special. Does it need intricate new cornices and skirting boards? Or new timber windows and doors to open up the space and add some detail to the room? Or would an exceptional paint colour or wallpaper do the job? What colours or fabrics could be used on old, outdated pieces of furniture to upcycle them and make them sing?

I believe that any room can be made to look and feel amazing; it's all in how you approach it and what you bring to the space. It's the combination of interesting elements that creates distinction. Think of it as like making a cake but not following the recipe perfectly: always throw a little something extra in to spice things up. In fact, I find myself feeling disappointed when a room I create comes together too perfectly – there's nothing I hate more than dull!

That said, avoid setting out to design a space in a completely haphazard way, as you will end up with a disjointed mess. To create a room that has lots of contradictory elements, which all work together, you have to begin with a clear plan. Most importantly, you must find one element that can unify the madness – for me, it's colour, but you might discover your own approach using pattern or texture. Get this right and you will be able to create a fabulous, interesting and inspiring space that truly reflects you, your family and all that you love.

ANTIQUES

Collecting antiques and incorporating them into your home adds sophistication and can help balance the use of bright colours and zany patterns on fabrics, wallpapers and art. When I have the time, I like nothing better than to spend a day out and about exploring auction houses, junk shops and antique stores, hunting for the perfect piece, whether for a client or for my own home. One-off items discovered this way can really make a room and help create that eclectic look I love so much. They also tend to be the pieces you love the most and can never let go of.

Collecting furniture, art or interesting pieces on your travels imbues them with emotion. We can look at a piece of furniture twenty years down the track and remember exactly where we bought it, how much we paid for it and the quirky person who sold it to us – the story of the piece will continue to bring us joy throughout our lifetime.

Something I always do when I am heading out to look for pieces, whoever they're for, is to make a list of all the items I need and the rough dimensions of each. Similarly, when embarking on a new project, I always make a spreadsheet to keep track of every piece purchased along the way – including how much I paid for it, its dimensions and a photograph. This information can be so useful: when it comes to placing the pieces into the floor plan; to keep a record of what you have already bought; and also for keeping track of your budget as you go along.

"Amid pleasures and palaces though we may roam, be it ever so humble, there's no place like home."

- John Howard Payne, 'Home Sweet Home', 1823

A GALLERY OF
CHILDREN

A.A. MILNE

ILLUSTRATIONS BY
H. WILLEBEEK LE MAIR

COLOUR & PATTERN PLAY

I have always been drawn to colour and pattern, and believe injecting both into a room can spark an instant sense of joy. Used well, they give an air of individuality and help create rooms that are full of energy. Layering a bold, multicoloured throw on the end of your bed, or selecting an array of mismatched cushions for your lounge room sofa, can be simple but effective ways of uplifting a space and making both you and your home feel fabulous and refreshed.

As the title of this chapter suggests, at its heart, the use of colour and pattern should be all about play. I love to experiment with colour, to push the boundaries and put interesting combinations together into a unique palette. Bucking at anything normal and coming up with something *extra*-ordinary is what gets my heart racing every single time. Whether you're mixing and matching period furniture with more modern elements, challenging expectations with daring colour and pattern combinations, or boldly covering a room head-to-toe in one pattern – walls, sofas, armchairs, cushions … everything – be confident and just do it!

Colour and pattern are everywhere in our daily lives. From an interesting colour palette in a streetscape, to a wonderful old wallpaper or luxuriously patterned vintage dress, inspiration is all around – you just need to open your eyes to it. Take photos of the combinations you see, make a note of those you are most drawn to, and use these as the starting point for putting together an interesting colour and pattern palette for your home.

One of the biggest secrets I can share for creating a home full of pattern and colour, is that colour can be the one ingredient, if used properly, that holds everything together. The way I unify seemingly mismatched furniture and patterns is by repeating or referencing colours from a similar palette within the space, even if those colours are unusual or otherwise unexpected.

Whether you love warmer or cooler tones, there must always be a balance when putting together colour and pattern. Choose an array of patterned and plain fabrics in your selected palette to use on various pieces in a room. Consider how much pattern you are happy to live with. If you prefer a more toned-down look, I suggest covering larger pieces of furniture in plain or ditsy fabrics (i.e. with small, irregular patterns), and covering accent pieces such as armchairs, ottomans and scatter cushions in bolder, more multicoloured patterns.

When I build schemes using colour and pattern, I often think of them as a big jigsaw puzzle. You have to make sure that each element works collectively in a cohesive yet interesting way, and fit the pieces together to create a wonderful overall result. Consider layering traditional florals with more modern geometric patterns, stripes or checks, and using a mix of large, medium and small pattern scales. Sometimes a clashing element, such as a bold multicoloured geometric pattern in a slightly 'off' colour, can be just what your room needs to conjure the unexpected. I like to look for patterns that I haven't seen used very often. This is part of the reason that I love to use antique textiles to cover ottomans, bedheads and cushions, or even as tablecloths or hanging works of art on a wall. Often one of a kind, these textiles add a special, cosy feeling to any room and often end up being pieces that are cherished for the rest of our lives.

Don't be afraid of colour and pattern. Embrace them and incorporate them into your home, even if you start with just one room. I guarantee you won't be able to stop, as it is super addictive once you start. Combining colour and pattern is the foundation to creating a comfortable home that is full of interest, happiness and unique style.

STRIVING FOR THE UNEXPECTED

A SPECIAL THING HAPPENS
WHEN A PARTICULAR,
WELL-THOUGHT-OUT,
BUT NEVER PREDICTABLE,
COMBINATION OF MATERIALS
COMES TOGETHER:

MAGIC

mOda

In my younger years, if ever I was asked what I wanted to do for a living, I would always reply, 'I'd like to be a fashion designer.' I used to read every *Vogue* magazine and I would paste tear sheets of cool fashion shoots and fabulous rooms I loved all over my bedroom walls – a wallpaper of my dream life, so to speak!

Fashion is something I am still intensely interested in. There is definitely crossover between designing a divine, interesting room and designing an exceptional dress; many of the same principles apply. Just as I like to create rooms that are always different, I love wearing clothes that nobody else wears, clothes that make people curious. What I wear is an expression of me. It can show who I am and what I am about. Therefore, most of the clothes I own are either vintage or are pieces I have had tailor-made. I believe the art of dressing well, as with dressing a room well, is in the combinations. For example, I may pare back a stand-out dress by combining it with an unusual vintage vest or an elegant blazer – it's about pulling together interesting pieces to create a totally individual look.

Recently, a lovely woman contacted me via Instagram, as she had a set of cool vintage curtains that she wanted to offer me. She'd had them made in the United Kingdom many years ago and had carried them with her all the way to Australia, but no longer needed them. Knowing my penchant for singular vintage fabrics, she thought I would love them. She was right! I bought the curtains from her and ended up making a fabulous dress out of them. People often ask me, 'Where did you get that amazing dress?' I love that it is one of a kind and that it is made out of recycled material that had been loved and cared for since the 1970s as curtains and is now loved as one of my favourite dresses.

Vintage fashion is such a wonderful concept. You don't have to go full-on vintage from head to toe, but by incorporating one or two pieces into your outfit – whether it's a coat, vest, earrings or a hat – you can make your outfit your own while at the same time supporting recycling. Whether upcycled or repurposed, fashion or furniture – vintage is great for the environment and creates fun, unrepeatable outfits and rooms.

When it comes to fashion, I am fastidious about fit. I think having something made to match you and your shape is really important and can make a big difference to the overall appearance of your outfit. Knowing what styles and cuts best suit your body shape is paramount. I'm lucky that my dearest friend, Sophie, is a dress designer, and I can always rely on her startling talent to make me something stunning and different that suits my shape perfectly. Since I started having most of my clothes made to fit, I now find it difficult to buy items off the rack. They never seem to fit well and always look 'wrong' somehow. Not to mention there's the added risk of turning up to an event wearing the same dress as someone else! If having your clothes custom-made is out of reach, consider taking a trusted friend shopping with you, to get a second opinion as to whether the fit of the piece you are considering is right for you.

CELEBRATING THE aRtisAn

One of the aphorisms I use most often is, 'Buy once, buy well'. This principle of quality over quantity really sums up what I'm all about. I'd prefer to have one outstanding, custom-made, quality sofa in a room with a couple of recycled antique armchairs upholstered in fabulous fabrics than two mass-produced beige linen sofas that will last about five years, if you're lucky.

Over the years, I have worked really hard to find the very best craftspeople – in Brisbane, Sydney and Melbourne – to carry out furniture building and upholstery work for me. To me, quality is paramount. I don't like to provide my clients with furniture that is produced in huge quantities on an assembly line, which is often poor quality and sold everywhere. Rather, I try to educate my clients as to the many benefits of investing in custom-made pieces or antiques that will last a lifetime. It never ceases to amaze me how long quality items can last with good care and maintenance.

I was recently invited by an old client to go to her home and look at her lounge room, as her sofa and armchair needed re-covering. The last time she had decorated the room was thirty years ago, and the sofa and armchair were just starting to tear in a few spots. Although it was clear some of the items needed re-covering after so much time and use, the room still looked fantastic. I couldn't believe she'd had thirty years' worth of life out of the furniture. I shouldn't have been surprised – it was custom-made for her using high-quality workmanship. It goes to show that while good-quality fabrics and custom-made furniture are more expensive in the short term, in the long run they far outlive the cheap, mass-produced alternatives and therefore are actually better value.

It's not just about longevity. Custom-made furniture offers unrivalled flexibility. Finding the perfect piece to suit a room and its owner becomes infinitely easier when you can have something made in almost any size and finished with any material. Whether it's choosing the right handwoven fabric or unique pattern to pull a room together, or designing the frame, filling and upholstery to suit the individual size and comfort requirements of the owner, the benefits of custom-made furniture are hard to beat.

I would love to see more artisanal manufacturing programs for young people in Australia, where they can learn the skills and methods of good old traditional manufacturing. When Sam and I first had the idea to create Anna Spiro Textiles, I wanted to use an Australian manufacturer to print the collection. At the time, there weren't many skilled hand screen-printers in Australia doing beautiful work. Fortunately, we found the best man for the job, and I believe the growth of our business has contributed to the growth of his. These dying trades need to be revived, supported and encouraged. If we don't pass on these traditional ways now, they may be lost forever.

Next time you are thinking of buying a sofa, armchair, lamp or piece of furniture from a furniture store, bear in mind that you may be buying just 'one of many' and in doing so supporting mass-production using cheap materials and labour. Instead, why not consider visiting a local vintage store, auction house or decorating store, and buying a reclaimed or antique piece of furniture. Or perhaps have a special custom-made piece manufactured by hand by a local tradesperson and covered in a gorgeous fabric. You will end up with something that is not only absolutely beautiful (to you, personally), but is exactly the size you need, fulfils all of your comfort requirements, is completely different to what your friends have, and is something that you will love and cherish for a very long time.

LIVING GENTLY SPARKS CREATIVITY

When I started my design business all those years ago, I was always in a hurry. My entire focus was on growing the business and taking on as many clients and projects as I could – which meant sacrificing many other things in my life. I worked excessively long days – and nights – and at the same time tried my hardest to be a great mum to my boys. Between my work and my children, there wasn't much time left for anything else. Life was hectic, and I'd often find myself burnt out and exhausted.

These days, I am still very busy with work and I really love what I do. The business continues to grow, and I am always excited by the many and varied projects we work on. However, I am more focused on creating a balanced life that allows me to spend more time on fewer projects and to live a little more gently. My priorities are my boys, my partner, my family and friends, exercise, healthy eating, looking after myself, going to the beach, trying to live well and enjoying my work. It took me a while to understand that if I'm not exercising or otherwise looking after myself, I can't be productive in all the other aspects of my life.

I'm also certain that the decision I made to spend more time living at the beach, immersed in the natural wonderland of Stradbroke Island, has helped my imagination to grow. What we imagine is shaped by what we see and experience all the time, and living by the beach is an incredible resource for my work. The colours I see there are so often the colours I combine in the rooms and homes I create, as well as being the ones that make me feel most happy and at peace.

Spreading yourself too thin across too many projects is never a good idea – I learnt that lesson the hard way. It is something I keep in the front of my mind every single day, so that I don't drop the ball and start saying yes to too many things. Nowadays, I want to put my everything into every project I take on, instead of taking on so many projects that each one only gets a tiny bit of me.

cOLLabORatIOn

Collaboration, I feel, works for everyone involved. It gives large companies the opportunity to work with new up-and-coming designers, or with established designers who have a large following; it puts designers' creativity prominently out there on the world stage; and it leads to products and outcomes for the end user that are exciting, unique and instantly desirable.

When designing a house from scratch or renovating an existing house, often the best results come when a client chooses to collaborate with both an architect and an interior designer. Some of my most rewarding projects have been those where I have worked closely with an architect to create a fabulous house for a client. One of the most gorgeous architects I've collaborated with is the Brisbane-based director of Marc&Co., Angus Munro. I worked with him on a house in New Farm, Queensland and the respect we had for each other's ideas and creative input the entire way through the design of the project was fantastic. This sort of strong architect–designer–client relationship is what can happen when each person is confident in themselves as a contributor to the project, while remaining open to the ideas of others. With the New Farm house, this dynamic, respectful approach directly resulted in a uniquely creative outcome for our clients.

Collaborating with big companies to create unique and interesting products can also be incredibly rewarding. In 2020, I launched the Anna Spiro Design rug collection with Australian company Designer Rugs. We created four beautiful designs, each offering something different: a modern geometric design (Otto), a more traditional botanical theme (Kandilli), and both a large- and small-scale floral motif (Flora). Ensuring flexibility for the buyer, by offering a mix of designs and styles, is something we were very conscious of when conceptualising the collection. Someone looking for a more modern look can opt for Otto, the geometric pattern, while a customer who loves florals or more traditional motifs can go for Kandilli or Flora. Creating designs that appeal to a wide range of people is so important when collaborating and creating products for retail.

Another great experience has been working with American company Anthropologie on an exciting product collaboration, which is due for release in spring of 2021. I have loved Anthropologie for as long as I can remember. I always visit their stores when I am in the United States, often bringing home some of their delightful patterned napery or small tableware items. When they approached me to create an Anna Spiro collection, I was quick to say yes. I think the partnership between us is perfect, as both our brands love and celebrate colour and pattern. My team and I created a number of patterns for Anthropologie to use across a varied collection of goods. There will be candles, notebooks, lamps and shades, and lots more wonderful and exciting pieces to collect in the range.

Another recent collaboration has been with world-renowned handpainted wallpaper company de Gournay. Together we created the truly special 'Island Garden' mural wallpaper, which has been painted on a gorgeous tea-stained rice paper. The design was inspired by my love of the beach and ocean generally, but also by a visit to the Great Barrier Reef in early 2020. A client had invited me up to Cairns to look at refitting their tourist boats in a colourful, patterned style. Unfortunately, due to the coronavirus pandemic, the project had to be postponed. Nevertheless, my three-day exploration of the reef and its myriad colourful fish and coral was more than enough to inspire my design for de Gournay. I chose to wrap the front sitting room of my new office–apartment with the Island Garden design and it is like being at the beach every day, living with the fish and other sea creatures under the water. Partnering with de Gournay was an absolute career highlight. Our mutual love for colour, pattern and high-quality workmanship resulted in a highly successful collaboration that I am extremely proud of.

To align, partner and collaborate with such well-respected worldwide companies has marked an exciting and pivotal stage in my career and has allowed me to explore my creativity even further. The experience and knowledge these partnerships have given me is intensely satisfying, as I love to learn about different industries and understand the intricacies of making beautiful things from scratch.

A CONSIDERED APPROACH

If you've read this far, it will probably come as no surprise to learn that I like to incorporate surprise elements in almost every room I create. However, to do this successfully it is important to maintain a sense of overall harmony in the design – or else you risk the whole thing falling flat.

Unfortunately, there is no hard and fast rule as to what makes a 'balanced' yet intriguing look. Self-editing is your best friend, but that skill doesn't come at the drop of a hat. Since the early years of my career, I have become better at editing and realising what works together in an interesting yet harmonious way – and what doesn't. While one must have some sort of natural flair to be a designer, of course, years of practice and real-life projects are what have really taught me to edit and refine my schemes, and ultimately to design spaces that are interesting but not overdone.

It's important to note here the difference between *clutter* and *collection*. The look I love and celebrate can sometimes be mistaken for a messy, cluttered look. I have had a few new clients tell me that they don't like clutter. Honestly, I dislike it too. But I adore collecting and incorporating interesting objects, art and furniture into my projects – especially items that have meaning to my clients.

Quite simply, clutter and curated collections are two completely different entities. Clutter is that meaningless stuff piled up in a disorderly way, the sort of thing that makes one feel untidy, anxious and disorganised. Of course, chaos and mess do not create a harmonious home! On the other hand, a carefully curated collection – consisting of *objets d'art* and rare pieces you have collected on your travels, arranged in an orderly, artful way throughout your home, mixed with other items of interest such as antique and modern art – can create a distinctive and very personal style. It comes back to adding a little bit of this, a little bit of that, and a sprinkle of something else, to achieve a perfectly balanced result. That's the secret to creating a wonderful, genuine look in a home: never too much of one thing, with every element curated and arranged with thought and consideration.

Although experience is the greatest guide, *originality* and *unity* are the two key concepts I keep in mind as I consider a design. That is, I always look to bring something new and different, something unexpected and wholly me, but I also consider ways to unify that wild side. I'm always looking for *that thing* that will pull the disparate elements together and create an aesthetic whole – whether it's a pattern that connects the room by incorporating all the different colours used, a single colour that complements the whole palette, or a plain fabric that calms a space.

À PARIS CHEZ — ANTOINETTE POISSON — Nº3

À PARIS CHEZ — ANTOINETTE POISSON — Nº16

LISA FINE

PORTER'S PAINTS

MONTPELIER STREET

JEAN MONRO

INSIDE TANGIER

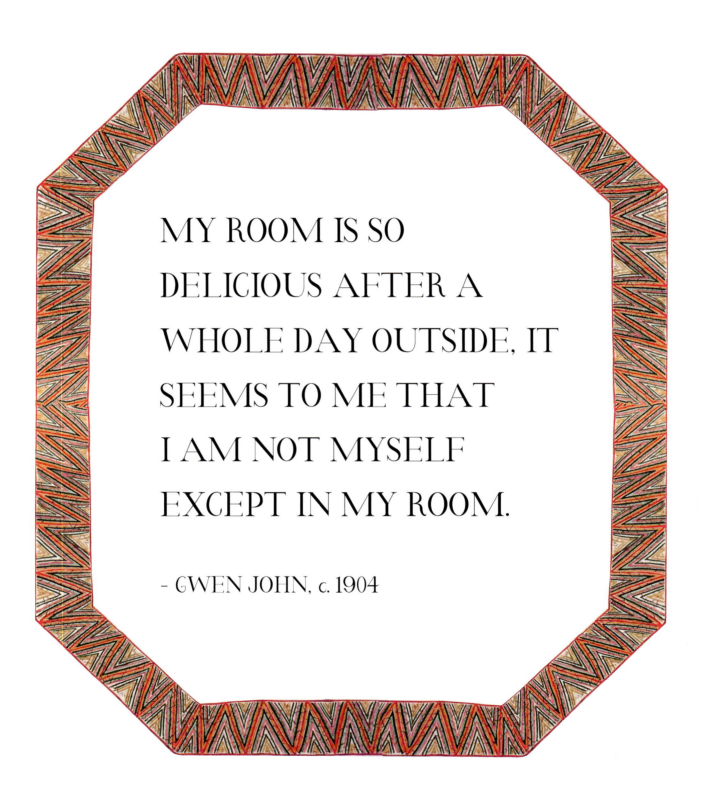

MY ROOM IS SO
DELICIOUS AFTER A
WHOLE DAY OUTSIDE, IT
SEEMS TO ME THAT
I AM NOT MYSELF
EXCEPT IN MY ROOM.

- GWEN JOHN, c. 1904

Making Magic

Design & Decoration

It's important to understand the difference between design and decoration. Design involves working in collaboration with an architect or draftsperson to create the interior space of a structure, room or building. This includes the selection of hard finishes such as flooring, joinery and wall finishes; cabinetry design; paint colours; and kitchen and bathroom layouts and finishes, including details like tiles, sanitaryware and feature lighting. Decorating, on the other hand, involves the furnishing of a space with throughtfully chosen furniture, textiles, art and accessories.

Anna Spiro Design offers both design and decoration services, because I find that starting from the very beginning of a project and carrying it right through to the end can result in something really exceptional. Getting a designer involved in a project as early as possible is truly a worthwhile investment, as it can help you sidestep some expensive mistakes. A good designer will help their client make well-informed decisions. Sometimes their suggestions can seem expensive, but they are inevitably a lot less costly than making a mistake and then having to do it all over again, the right way.

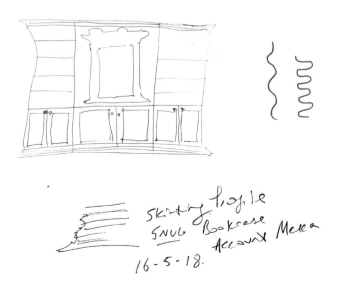

CLIENT TRUST

The importance of mutual trust between designer/decorator and client cannot be overstated. Clients who have the confidence to trust their designer will get the best results. Having a team – and that includes the client – that works together collaboratively and respectfully is key, as it sets everyone at ease. This sense of ease is critical. For a designer, understanding a client's wishlist of wants, needs and loves from the outset is integral to any successful project, but that can be hard to achieve if there are reservations on either side. Trust breeds confidence, which injects essential energy into the design and decoration process.

If I sense a client can't quite trust me, I get a bit anxious. Consequently, they end up not getting the best of me because I'm second-guessing myself all the way through the process. Working under that sort of pressure can result in a project turning out to be rather ho-hum and often not well curated. A lack of trust tends to lead to picking and pulling at every turn, which can not only be extremely frustrating for both parties, but can result in a project that is lacklustre and feels disjointed or unbalanced, leaving everyone unhappy with the end result.

When I go to my dentist or my accountant, I tell them what I need and, although I ask lots of questions, I trust them to give me good, solid advice and do the right thing for me. It's the same when you ask a designer to help design a house: tell them what you'd love to achieve, ask questions, but trust them – this is what they do every single day. If you choose a great designer whose work you love, they will provide you with an amazing outcome that you will want to live with for a very long time.

Escalated
time frame
MUST be completed
pre-Xmas

European Pinch Pleat
Heading, 2 times fullness
on an A.S. Custom mounted
curtain Rod.

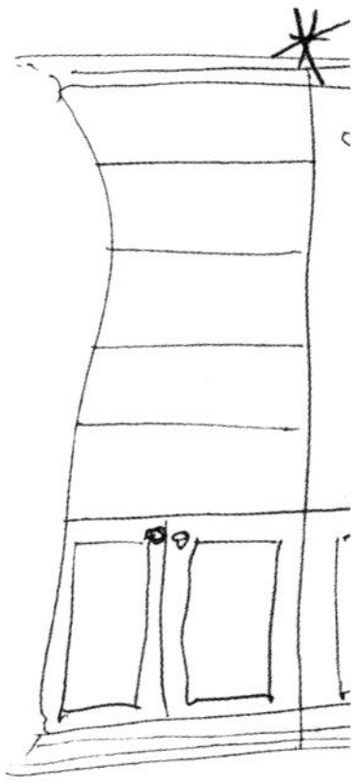

*150mm - 200mm Horizontal VJ

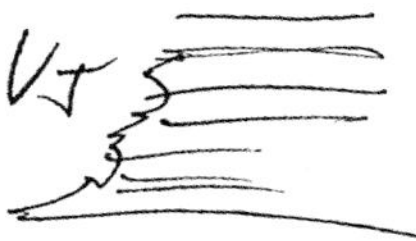

Husband
obsessed with
lust v. → How can
we HIDE IT!!

Skirting Profile
SNUG Bookcase
Account Mella

16-5-18.

*150mm - 200mm Horizontal VJ on all

Floor Plan Layout
Account - SALTER

English
Sofa

Curtains
Armchairs x2

Fireplace

Built-in
Bookcase

Georgian
Sofa table

ART

French
doors -
Curtains over

All Furniture to
sit on Sisal
Rug over Timber
Floors

Lounge Shades A/c - fing

T- 6 inch
B - 14 inch
H - 12 inch
With a 2 inch AR

Rebate on Bookcase
doors to be 12mm

*150mm - 200mm Horizontal VJ

Fabric for
Bedskirt
ABT Penola Navy
with pleats on corners,
top Borders & Lined
(Allow for Interlining)

Husband
obsessed with
lust v. → How can
we HIDE IT!!

Fabric for
Bedskirt
ABT Penola Navy
with pleats on corners,
top Borders & Lined
(Allow for Interlining

Escalated
time frame
MUST be completed
pre-Xmas

Skirting Profile
SNUG Bookcase
Account Mella

16-5-18.

16-5-18.

Rebate on Bookcase
doors to be 12mm

DESIGN PROCESS

The design phase is a critical stage in any project, as it sets the background and scene for the decoration and furnishings of the house or room. If a designer is involved from the outset, they are able to shape the space to suit the style of decoration that will eventually follow – which can make an enormous difference to the overall finish and look of a home. When regarding a potential space, a designer will consider what structural elements may help to take your project to the next level. They may, for example, add panelling to provide texture and interest in a hallway; pull out a wall to increase light and space; or adjust the placement of windows so they won't negatively affect the positioning of furniture (the bed in a bedroom, or a sofa or bookshelf in a lounge room). The designer's insight allows for crucial groundwork to be laid, leading to results that could never be achieved without that professional input.

It's hard to overstate how important it is to choose your design team wisely. Interview the architects and designers you are considering and make a decision based on your gut feeling. Ask yourself: Will they help me achieve the results I want, or will they push me in all the wrong directions? Do I like the look of some or all of the projects they have completed in their portfolio? As a designer myself, I believe I should try to push my clients to new heights, but I understand that it is equally necessary to consider how they live, what they want in a home and what they love to be surrounded by. A good designer will always have these things in mind, and as such can help you achieve the outcome you are seeking.

Ralph's

PORTERS
PAINTS

AMALFI

BOX SKY

FLAME

MYKONOS

Thai silk

PARIS

ANNA SPIRO

...must let go
...e life we
...planned,
...to accept
...ne that is
...ng for us."

TENNISON
...an and Geoff Newberry's restored English rectory

Facing page: Angela Junklow and her
daughters, Daphne and Veronica, on
the porch of their Los Angeles home, designed by Timothy Corrigan. The living room features a sofa hand-made in
Christopher Hyland fabric and covered Plexiglass armchairs from J.F.
Chen, and Balinese sculpture. The
Aga John area rug was designed by Corrigan, and the mini cocktail table
is from the 1940s. See Resources.

When embarking on any project, a strong brief is essential. Whether that means having an open conversation with your chosen design team, or drawing up plans for smaller or personal projects, don't set off without knowing (at least broadly) where you want to go and what you want to achieve. Making sure that your designer and architect are informed of any style likes and dislikes, and are aware of the various components you want in your home, will help them understand your personal taste and overall vision for the project. Discussing a budget for the work is one of the most important tasks at this early stage.

When renovating, often a big part of what is needed is simply a different way of thinking about the existing property. It is useful to consider the property/site in its raw, untouched state to get a good sense of place. Alongside your designer, examine the surrounds, observe where the light comes from, note the placement of trees on the property, etc. Without this initial assessment, you risk creating a home that feels out of place or intangibly wrong. In the same vein, consider what can be used and salvaged from the site. Ripping everything out to begin with a clean slate can remove a building's character and quirk – not to mention, such historic details tend to be the hardest and most expensive to reproduce if you change your mind later. I am always searching for what can be kept. Making new additions obviously has its place, but using old elements as an asset and reworking what you already have help maintain the underlying character and charm of a place – and keep your budget on track.

After visiting a site and receiving the client's brief and budget, a designer will often create a 'storyboard' to get the initial design phase started – essentially a picture book proposing how the house/ room could look and feel. This initial concept usually includes lots of indicative imagery, some fabric/wallpaper swatches, colour ideas and rough sketches. It's a useful tool to ensure everyone is on the same page, as most clients need images and sketches to really begin to visualise what is being proposed. This storyboard is often used as a reference point right the way through a project, guiding the team's ideas as they develop and helping the client understand and envision the overall aesthetic. In your own personal projects, creating a scrapbook or pinboard of the things you love – and the things you really don't – will help you narrow down the look and style you want to achieve.

Once the initial concept is approved, the design development stage can begin, wherein highly detailed schematic drawings and specification documents are drawn up in alignment with the plans provided by the architect or draftsperson. During this stage, design ideas are formalised, and the client is involved in making any changes or additions. The focus here is squarely on the details: from developing room layouts, making lighting selections and choosing wall and floor finishes, to ensuring cabinetry designs are both practical and aesthetically pleasing, and window and door designs work within the framework of the project. Once all of this work is completed and the client is happy with the drawings, layouts, finishes and selections, the project is ready to be sent to tender.

The designer's work isn't finished yet, though. Sometimes the best-laid plans can be thrown off kilter once you're on site and the build has started. Things can look very different on paper, so it's important for the designer to be on hand to make revisions and decisions along the way. One element I always ensure I look at on site is paint colour. I put a lot of thought and effort into choosing paint colour combinations and often use an array of precisely selected hues, with some rooms having three or four different colours – on walls, skirting boards, architraves, doors, decorative details, etc. It is imperative to test your paint colours in the rooms in which they are going to be used, as the light in the space will have a big impact on the overall finished look of the painted room.

Towards the end of the build stage – as cabinetry, lighting and hardware start to be installed, paints are applied and things begin to feel like they are coming together – it can be easy to second-guess the choices and selections that have been made, as they may not look right … yet! Although the finished result might seem near, it's still so far away. Stay confident. This is not the time to worry. Remember, it's not until the very end, once all the elements – including fabrics, wallpapers, furniture and soft furnishings – are in place that all the dots finally get joined up and you can see the full magic at play!

DECORATING
PROCESS

THE NEW AUSTRALIAN GARDEN

KIT KEMP *EVERY ROOM TELLS A STORY*

VICTOR HUGO IN E
villa of the man behind L

THE WORLD OF
INTERIORS

SUNBURST CHATEAU:
A French manor's sparkling restoration

VERAN
easy living
SUNNY
SPACES &
GREAT
ESCAPES

STAGE 1: CONCEPT

Whether you're decorating as part of a large renovation or new build, or redecorating an existing home – or even just freshening up one room – the process always starts with deciding on an overall look and feel. As with the early design stage, this usually means creating a concept or storyboard that captures the style of decoration and furnishings you plan to use. This initial concept should cover both the overarching style and the design details. If you are using a professional decorator, you should be offered a few options at the first concept presentation (at Anna Spiro Design we generally propose two distinct concepts). This fosters collaboration and allows the client to choose which style they want developed further.

When decorating a space, there are myriad factors at play: scale, balance, comfort, colour, pattern, function, space, proportion, detail and – one of my favourites – offbeat elements. It is the decorator's job to bring together and balance all of these. Planning is essential, of course, but sometimes elements just fall into place naturally and holistically; some things cannot be planned – and these serendipitous moments should be relished. Overthinking, swapping options in and out, and constantly changing your mind, can result in a lack of cohesion and a project that just doesn't turn out 'right'. Often the first idea is the best one to focus on and develop.

'TO A LADY WHO, LOOKING AT AN ENGRAVING OF A HOUSE, CALLED IT AN UGLY THING, HE SAID, "NO, MADAM, THERE IS NOTHING UGLY; I NEVER SAW AN UGLY THING IN MY LIFE: FOR LET THE FORM OF AN OBJECT BE WHAT IT MAY - LIGHT, SHADE AND *PERSPECTIVE* WILL ALWAYS MAKE IT BEAUTIFUL."'

- JOHN CONSTABLE, QUOTED IN CR LESLIE, *MEMOIRS OF THE LIFE OF JOHN CONSTABLE*, 1843

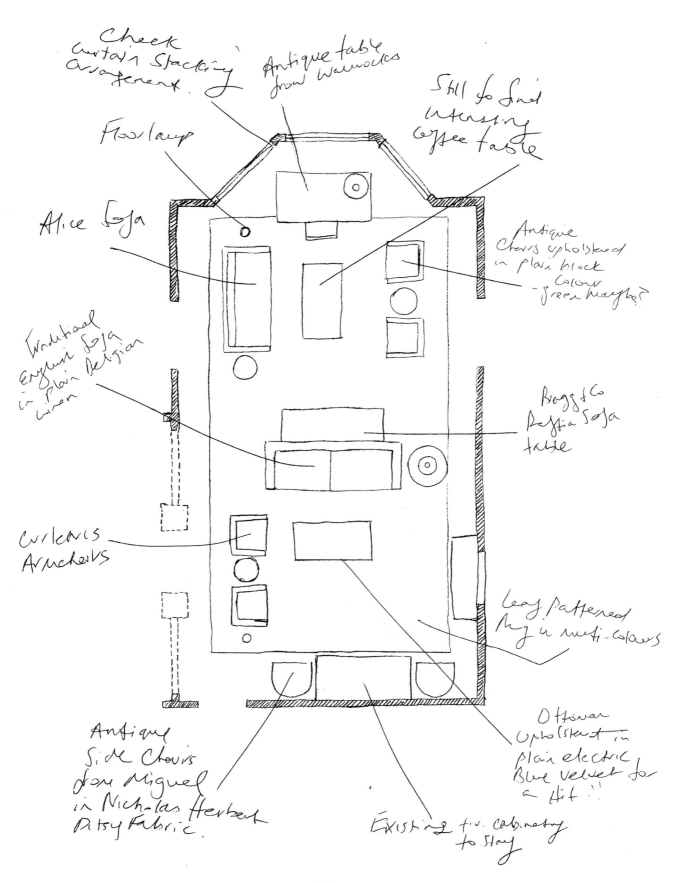

Check curtain stacking arrangement.

Antique table from Warnocks

Still to find interesting coffee table

Floor lamp

Alice Sofa

Antique chairs upholstered in plain block colour - green maybe?

Traditional English Sofa in plain Belgian linen

Briggs & Co Raffia Sofa table

Curtains Armchairs

Leaf Patterned rug in multi-colours

Antique side chairs from Miguel in Nicholas Herbert Ditsy Fabric.

Existing t.v. cabinetry to stay

Ottoman upholstered in plain electric blue velvet for a hit !!

I generally start my storyboard by selecting the fabrics I intend to use. The patterns and colours form an instant overall feeling and vibe. Selecting a 'trophy' fabric, which features all the colours I want to use in the room, is often a great starting point. After allocating the trophy fabric, I then bring in other fabrics – patterns, textures and plains – that I feel will work well with the multicoloured trophy fabric. Sometimes I will put the hero fabric on the smallest piece of furniture, so that it doesn't look too overwhelming in the space. Subtly referencing this bold fabric elsewhere in the room – for example, by using a few plain textiles in the least pronounced tones of the trophy fabric – can make for an exceptionally interesting and unexpected result.

Following fabric choice, I begin on the proposed furniture layout, which includes selection of the various sofa, armchair and ottoman styles I am contemplating for the room. At this stage I also like to consider any antiques I might want to use and any new pieces that will need to be made. I love working out interesting furniture placement plans and like to position furniture in a conversational way. Often the rooms I create have only one sofa, which anchors the space, along with an assortment of armchairs in different styles and fabrics. I think people generally prefer sitting in an armchair, whereas sofas are more for lounging and lying down on. In addition, armchairs can be moved around more readily and can make a room feel more comfortable and eclectic.

When I am decorating numerous rooms in a home, I like to use elements that can be interchanged between rooms. For example, selecting fabrics in similar colour palettes throughout the overall concept can allow for pieces to be moved in and out of rooms over the course of time. This sort of flexibility can be of huge value to clients, as it stops spaces feeling outdated or tired, and allows for freshness when needed.

It is important to note that works of quality take time to produce. In today's world, it's easy to forget what actually goes into making something from scratch. Be wary of pushing to have things made in unrealistic timeframes, as the end result will always suffer. Just relax and enjoy the delicious suspense of waiting for that perfect piece to arrive. As my mother continues to remind me, 'Good things come to those who wait'.

Once the concept has been approved by the client, the decorator will prepare an itemised quotation including the cost of each item to be made, purchased and installed in the home, and their fees for managing the project from start to finish.

STAGE 2:
PROJECT MANAGEMENT

Although project management is truly integral to the second stage of the decorating process, a good project manager should be a mainstay of the design team from start to finish, particularly on bigger projects. They help generate and manage timeframes for the entire project, as well as organise the ordering and manufacture of all design elements – ultimately, they put all the well-laid plans into action.

I must admit, project management is not my strong point. As the creative director of my business, my time and energy are best spent in the first stage, formulating and preparing concepts with my design assistant. Fortunately, I can trust my two wonderful, experienced project managers to keep every project running like clockwork from start to finish. Regular updates (even bi-weekly at times) throughout the installation process keep everyone, including the client, involved and advised of any delays, ensuring the project stays on track. Good communication allows everyone to do their work in the most time-efficient way, without putting pressure on the designers, makers and tradespeople.

When you're aiming to create something extraordinary, the effort involved in bringing your ideas to fruition can be extreme. Due to the highly detailed nature of the work we do at Anna Spiro Design, it isn't just about ordering finished pieces from this or that company. Each bespoke item must be broken down into the individual elements required to have it made. If we're producing an armchair, for example, we need to: calculate the amount of fabric needed for the body and trim, and order it (or arrange printing if it's a unique pattern); order the chair frame to exact specifications (including frame width, seat height and swell, back height, arm width and height, edging detail, leg style, leg colour, infill, and so on); arrange for the chair to be upholstered; and, critically, ensure that the finished product is absolutely flawless.

We are so particular about achieving perfection that we arrange for all the fabrics and trims to be sent to our office so that we can cut them to size ourselves and double-check that all is in order before sending them off to be made into the final pieces. This sort of quality assurance is paramount when working with fine fabrics and bespoke furnishings, and is essential to the overall finish of a project. All the way through, we check, double check, triple check ... With so many balls in the air, good systems and organisation are absolutely crucial.

Once all of the items are ready, we organise installation. Usually this happens over the course of a few days for a small project, but it can take a few weeks for larger ones. Working with multiple contractors to install finishing elements such as wallpaper, curtains, feature lighting, rugs, furniture and art is a complex process, and it is best to book everyone well in advance so that work can be completed within the timeframe allocated.

A decorator's work should never be underestimated or thought of as glamorous. There's no high-heel culture in my office. We all wear flats or sneakers – footwear for a team that never sits down. For us, no detail is too small. With most of our projects, we even go so far as to select the bedding. We have elegant handmade sheets and quilt covers produced with detailing to match the colours we have used in the room, making them

very special and totally unique. On installation day, we steam the bed valances, curtains and loose fabric items, iron the sheets and make up all of the beds, so that our clients can feel the true luxury of sleeping in a well-made bed in an exceptionally presented house. Every last meticulous detail is considered. That is how you make a beautiful home.

A few weeks after installation, we send our clients a comprehensive booklet on how to care for their new furniture. This is a kind of bible that we are continuously adding to. It is an excellent resource that helps our clients understand how and when to arrange the upkeep and maintenance of their furniture, and who to use for the job. Quality items need to be looked after and properly maintained if they are to last well into the future: it's a fact of life.

THE
GRAND
FINALE

Room by Room

ROOMS

The rooms in a house combine to create a sanctuary. How you choose to design and decorate the spaces within your home is a wholly personal process; one that involves making numerous important decisions that will make the home as aesthetically pleasing, practical, cosy and comfortable as possible. Above all, your goal should be to create an environment that is reflective of you, your life and taste. Collect art, furniture and other items that have meaning to you. Surround yourself with all the things that you love and you'll be well on your way to making a home that is your favourite place on Earth.

SITTING ROOM

At home, the sitting room is where we come together. It should feel comfortable, inviting, exciting and beautiful. When preparing a design, I ask my clients, 'How do you want to feel in this room? What are the most important things to achieve?' The answer is almost always: comfort.

In order to build great comfort in a sitting room, it is important to consider the requirements of each member of the family: such as deeper sofas for taller people, and higher seats for older people. Using more armchairs and fewer sofas helps to achieve a mix of comfort options for all. Carefully considered fabric choices are another must for creating comfort – there is nothing worse than sitting in a chair upholstered in a prickly fabric or being stifled by a velvet-covered sofa on a humid day!

Overall, a sitting room should invite you and your guests in, wrap you up and make you want to linger for hours.

Fire mantle

Side Chair

Bobble Lamp

Decorative Urns

Glass Knot

Side Table

Gateleg Table

Sofa

Curtains

Curtains

Books

Ottoman

Floor lamp

DINING ROOM

With the trend towards open-plan living, most new houses no longer include a traditional dining room. Considering most dining rooms don't get daily use, the question has to be asked: is a formal dining room a waste of space?

Personally, if space isn't a problem, I love to incorporate a designated dining room. Even in a smaller home, I might justify its inclusion by considering that the room can have a dual purpose – it will be wonderful for hosting memorable dinner parties and family gatherings, of course, but it can also act as a workspace. With that in mind, it's important to choose dining room furniture that is both comfortable and aesthetically pleasing. I encourage buying an antique dining table and will often pair it with upholstered dining chairs, as I find them to be the most comfortable for lengthy periods. An upholstered dining chair also gives you the opportunity to use a fabulous fabric in the space. Another look that can be fun – and is often more economical – is using a variety of mismatched chairs, which can be collected over a period of time.

There are relatively few elements we can include in a dining room to make it look and feel exciting. Why not consider having a bit of fun and thinking outside of the box with your decoration: wallpapered walls, patterned curtains or an amazing rug are just a few ways you can let your creativity loose.

Curtains

Dutch Chandelier

Lambsbone
End Chairs

Antique Dining
Table

Candlesticks

Lamp

Dining chair

BEDROOM

One's bedroom should feel cosy and peaceful. I spend a lot of time in my bedroom and find that it's the one place I truly feel at ease. Therefore, it's a room that should be decorated in a way that contributes to a feeling of calm. One of the first things I ask my clients when helping them decorate their bedrooms is, 'What is your absolute favourite colour, the one you love to be surrounded by?' I want them to be submerged in a colour that makes them feel wonderful, safe and happy when they're in their bedroom. For me, blue is the colour that makes me happiest – any shade will do – perhaps because it reminds me of the ocean. In my bedroom in the city I have painted all the walls the most heavenly blue and the ensuite bathroom is tiled in aqua glass tiles.

Once you have settled on a colour for the bedroom, it's time to think about what sort of bed you would like. Choosing the right mattress is key to creating a restful room. We spend a lot of time in bed, so select a mattress that is the most comfortable you can afford. Quality bedlinen also contributes to the comfort of a bedroom. Personally, I prefer to sleep between high-thread-count cotton sheets, especially living in humid Queensland. And remember: it's worth putting a little extra time and care into making up your bed – there's nothing more luxurious than ironed sheets.

Bedside tables are another item people are particular about, and practicality is often the most important factor my clients want us to consider. Some people like drawers, some like shelves, and some just need a small table. I like mismatched bedside tables and mostly opt for antique pieces. If space permits, a larger bedside table, such as a chest of drawers, is not only aesthetically pleasing but also very practical.

A sitting area can be a nice addition to a bedroom if there's space. Alternatively, a bedroom chair or bed-end stool can make a room feel more comfortable.

Alice Sofa

Antique Chest

Bedhead

Lamp

Bed-end Bench

Bedside

Armchair

Rug

KITCHEN

The kitchen is the centre of any home – it's where we spend time cooking, eating and being together. I adore a big eat-in style kitchen, where the cabinetry hugs the perimeter of the room and a centre table is used for eating, congregating and preparing food. It's important to incorporate seating when designing a kitchen from scratch. For the cook, it's lovely to have company in the kitchen when preparing meals – good seating will encourage people to mill around.

I highly recommend installing a purpose-built butler's pantry if the space and budget allow – ideally with a spare oven, sink and dishwasher. With the busy lives we all lead, it's nice to be able to hide the day-to-day mess in the pantry, so that the main area of the kitchen can be clutter-free.

Incorporating unusual accessories and furniture into a kitchen design is a sure way to add some distinction. An antique Georgian plate stand, say, or an old butcher's block, can instantly make a kitchen feel charming and interesting. A sea of cabinetry can sometimes look rather dull, so why not use an antique armoire as a pantry cupboard? These sorts of unexpected inclusions can really add personality, as well as practicality, to your kitchen.

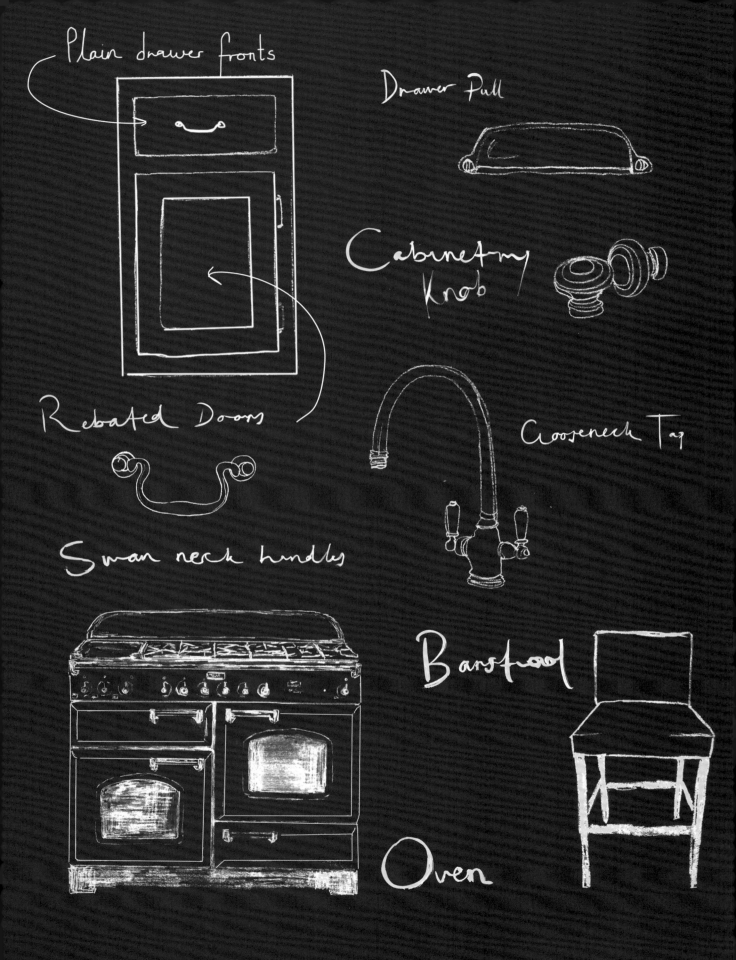

Plain drawer fronts

Drawer Pull

Cabinetry Knob

Rebated Doors

Gooseneck Tap

Swan neck handles

Barstool

Oven

BATHROOM

A bathroom should feel layered and furnished, not clinical. Incorporating pedestal basins, antique chests of drawers for storage, and old mirror-fronted wall cabinets can offer up lots of variety. Alternatively, a well-designed bathroom vanity can be both practical and a charming, unique piece of furniture – painting it a vibrant colour can really uplift the space.

A bath is a must for me, as is having an armchair nearby, so that my partner can sit and chat to me while I am in the tub. It's such a luxury to spend time soaking, floating and chatting. The other thing I usually incorporate, when space permits, is a shower room wrapped in floor-to-ceiling tiling – I love the feeling of privacy and peacefulness that a shower room provides, compared to a glass-walled shower. Having a discrete shower also makes the bathroom feel more like a room in its own right, which is my ultimate design goal.

Wall Light

Door Lever

Side Chair

Tulu Mirror

Bath

Shower

Pedestal Basin

Vanity Taps

Bath Tap

ENTRANCE HALL

Although rarely considered significant, or even 'rooms' per se, entryways and hallways can take you on an exciting journey if decorated in an intriguing way.

The entry is often neglected when it comes to interior design. However, it is the first port of call for any guests, so it pays to make it interesting. It should show visitors a snippet of what the rest of your home (if they are invited in) will look like. I often choose to hang beautiful art in this space, and include an antique hall table with lamps and shades covered in a fabric that complements the selected art pieces. If space allows, I tend to add side chairs (generally antique and upholstered in a fabric that provides some colour and pattern) on either side of the entrance table – I'm always looking to find diverse uses for furniture throughout a home, and these chairs can act as spares when you have more guests than you can cater for with your dining chairs. Arranging a personal collection, or some family photographs in elegant old silver frames, on top of the table can make a lovely addition and help to create a happy personal aesthetic.

As with entryways, hallway design can feel like an afterthought. Hallways are often left plain, white and, frankly, boring. People forget that the hallway is the artery that conveys us into the heart of the home. I love to give a hallway real character. Why settle for something uninteresting? You might decide to paint the walls and ceiling that wild colour you weren't quite confident enough to use in the dining room. Hall runners and interesting wall lights or feature ceiling pendants can also add interest to an otherwise bland space. I think it's nice to hang family photographs along the hallway – not so much as an obvious design feature, but rather for the family living in the home to enjoy as they pass through each day.

Console

Side Chair

Decorative

Mirror

Lamp

Books

Bust

Decorative Urns

Antique Boxes

UTILITY ROOM

The utility or laundry room is a space that isn't often given much thought. While for many people it may be last on their list of priorities, for me it is right at the top. I truly believe that creating a practical yet aesthetically pleasing utility room is essential to feeling organised and happy in your home.

Decorating this otherwise mundane room in a delightful way can make performing life's menial tasks, like washing and ironing, a pleasure. It's important to devote some of your time and budget to planning the layout, but also to think about how the room – including fittings, finishes and storage solutions – can be both functional and attractive. For clients, I often opt for stylish cabinetry finishes and skirted sections under worktops, distinctive tiling on floors and thoughtfully positioned hooks and shelves. Cane baskets and attractive laundry hampers add to the overall finished look. I challenge you to think seriously about your utility room and make it beautiful and practical. Trust me, it will change your life!

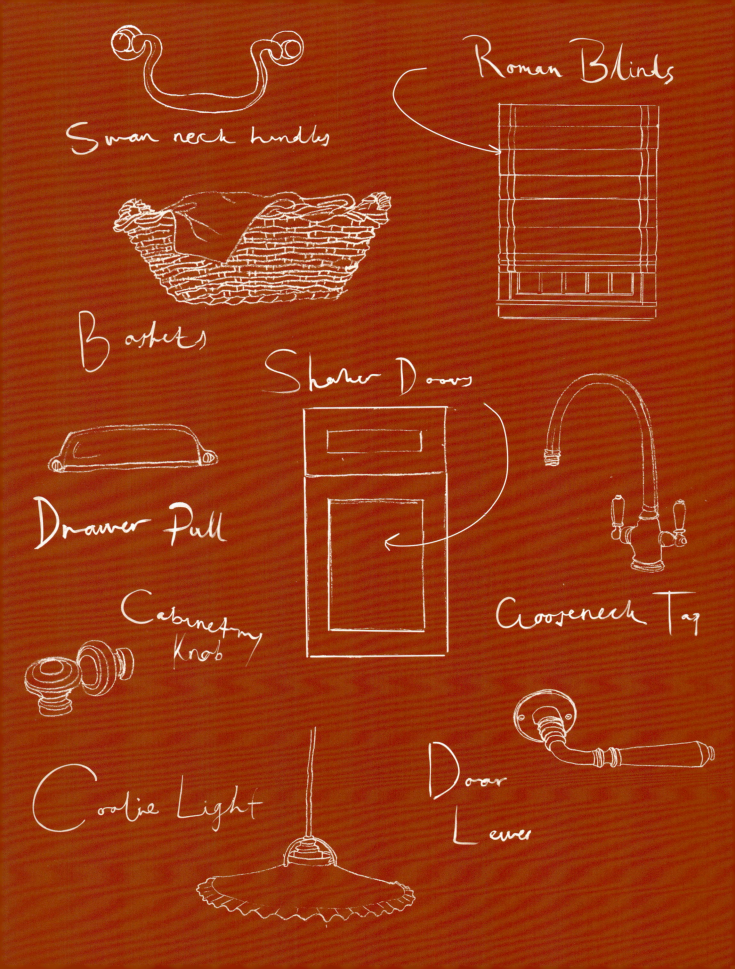

Swan neck handles

Roman Blinds

Baskets

Shaker Doors

Drawer Pull

Gooseneck Tap

Cabinetry Knob

Coolie Light

Door Lever

pRojects

of nOte

cHarLMoNT

The brief I was given by my clients for their home at Hamilton in Brisbane was for a 'toned down' version of what I normally do. They wanted a refined look in soft tones that incorporated antiques, art, outstanding custom-made furniture and a mix of plain and quiet-patterned fabrics. This brief really excited me, as it offered me a chance to create something different by reigning in my usual bright and bold style to create a sophisticated home for my clients that represented everything they loved.

This project came across my table right as COVID-19 hit around the world. While a number of our other projects were temporarily put on hold as we all grappled with what impacts the pandemic would have, these clients pressed ahead. The easing of my workload allowed me to work without disruption on this job over the Easter week, designing all the room schemes and selecting paint colours.

Although the look was to be more pared back than my usual style, it actually took me a lot more time, thought and work to get it right. It made me realise that my natural ability lies in amassing a great number of patterns and elements, and making them come together in an interesting way. So when I was asked to strip that whole process back, it posed a real challenge. Going against my natural tendency towards complex layering, and creating a room that was simpler in its design and execution, wasn't as easy as I had thought it would be. After working very hard to get the project concepts just right, we presented the entire scheme to the clients. Excitingly, they loved it all and we were given the go-ahead.

The formal sitting room and dining room, which flow into each other, are my favourite rooms in the house, representing a successful collaboration of colour, pattern and texture. We chose a mellow pale-green colour for the walls in the sitting room and a soft blue for the dining room. We linked the two areas together by selecting a beautiful, refined Michael Smith patterned fabric for the curtains in both rooms. A plain off-white linen sofa anchors the sitting room, while various accent chairs and stools are covered in either block colours or simple small checks, pinstripes and tone-on-tone patterns. A multicoloured rug is the trophy piece of the space, along with a painting by artist Bronte Leighton-Dore that we selected to hang above the fireplace. These elements pull together all the other components to create the magic in the room. The double-ended floorplan we opted for makes the space feel full and welcomes people in to sit, lounge, gather and be together.

SLIM AARONS · LA DOLCE VITA
FLORA· DIANA HAUTE BOHEMIANS

Throughout the house we selected soft blues and greens as the dominant colours, but introduced others as we worked through the various rooms, to add interest and variety. The family room and TV room are interconnected, so we worked the same fabrics into both areas to make them feel like one large space. A Sally Lee Anderson painting hangs above the sofa in the family room and brings together all the colours in the room – the red it adds into the space connects perfectly with the floral Flora Soames fabric we used for the cushions.

In the master bedroom, we wanted to create a room that felt cosy, comfortable and peaceful. We opted for a natural and off-white colour palette, and layered various textures together, including: a grass-weave wallpaper that wraps all the walls; a plush, custom-made wall-to-wall rug we designed ourselves; and a taupe and white vine-patterned Turnell & Gigon fabric for the curtains. A rare pair of matching antique bedside tables, which we purchased from local antique dealer Jessica Wallrock of Wallrocks Antiques, were the perfect find for the room in terms of scale, style and finish. The end result is a space that feels very calm and luxurious.

Downstairs, the brief was to design a children's hang-out room that would stand the test of time – and lots of wear and tear. We chose hard-wearing fabrics for the large upholstery pieces and accented them with patterned fabrics on cushions and lampshades. The colour palette references the garden outside and when the doors are flung open the entire space feels fresh, open and relaxed.

What we created at Charlmont is a look that will endure. It is sophisticated yet comfortable, and feels like a home that will always welcome family and friends with open arms. I am extremely proud of the interior I designed here and relished the challenge of doing something a little bit different. My clients trusted that I could provide them with a home they would love, and it was a joy to work with them to do just that.

iLuKA

Our client and his family purchased Iluka, at Sorrento on the Mornington Peninsula in Victoria, in early 2016 as a holiday house. The property was handed over in a significantly run-down state, having previously been owned by the same family for nearly ninety years. However, its potential gleamed brightly, its character-filled bones forming a strong starting point for renovation. For one, its enviable location on the beach at Sorrento is magical and takes your breath away upon arrival. The tall pine trees planted along the edge of the garden, where the grass leads down to the sand, create an atmosphere of majesty and charm. I am filled with delight every time I arrive at Iluka, both because of what I achieved there – it remains one of my stand-out projects to date – and the eminent sense of history and location.

The client's brief was to rework the interior floor plan of the existing cottage to cater for his extended family, who would be visiting often, and add a five-bedroom, five-bathroom extension – all the while being respectful of the long history of the place. For that reason, he wanted to ensure the new extension would be invisible from the beach side of the character-filled cottage. In addition, every new element was to be sympathetic and in keeping with the style of the original house.

Talented Melbourne architect Drew Cole was called in to design the structure of the new wing and help rework the interior floor plan of the existing house. My team and I were given creative and aesthetic reign over the project. We worked closely with Drew and his colleagues to design a number of traditional elements, such as the internal and external timber joinery, doors, a spectacular spiral staircase leading to the charming attic, wall panelling, marble thresholds, fireplace surrounds, cabinetry, trims and details. We used imported antique tiles from Europe on the bathroom floors and converted antique chests of drawers into bathroom vanities. Beautiful fabrics and wallpapers were selected and imported from across the globe – from textile and design houses such as Michael S. Smith, Soane, GP & J Baker, Rose Cumming, Décors Barbares and Pierre Frey, to name just a few.

We chose lights from Jamb and Vaughan Designs in London, and also sourced antique lighting. Ebony door handles (also from a maker in London) and handmade brass cabinetry pulls were used throughout. Basins, toilets and unlacquered brass taps were ordered from The English Tapware Company, along with a very special antique marble bath for the master bedroom's ensuite, which had to be craned into the house and the floor reinforced where the bath was to be positioned.

Every piece of furniture for the house was either custom-made by a highly skilled Australian artisan, or was an antique sourced at auction or through a dealer. A circa 1750s Georgian oak dresser-base, which I used as a hall table in the old section of the cottage, shows off its age by dipping in the middle. Not everyone would understand its beautiful imperfection, but I had admired the piece for some time and was delighted to finally find it a perfect home. It came from friend and antique dealer Martin Allen in Melbourne, along with a number of other exceptional pieces, which we dotted throughout the house.

The central bench in the kitchen, which was custom-made by renowned Melbourne furniture maker Robert Brown, was based on an old English pastry bench. Robert left no stone unturned in ensuring the overall proportion, finish and decorative detailing matched the original style perfectly.

We imported textiles from Britain, mainland Europe and America to make bespoke curtains, bedheads, sofas and armchairs. The Oscar de la Renta palm fabric used in one of the guest bedrooms is a standout, as are the Carolina Irving fabrics used to line wardrobe doors and internal doors for that little added charm.

Every element of the house was considered in meticulous detail and every part of the design was executed with integrity, always respecting and embracing traditional methods. For example, the cabinetry was constructed using solid natural timber, handpainted on the outside but left unpainted (instead oiled) on the inside. It's the most beautiful way of making cabinetry in my opinion, and the timber ages gracefully with time.

Every tradesperson involved in the project was working at the top of their game and they all seemed to share a strong sense of pride in being part of such a rare project. Builder Peter Anderson ensured the entire process ran like clockwork and wouldn't sign off on a single element until we were happy with it.

Being presented with a project such as Iluka, and being allowed to work with no restraint, was a singularly special opportunity for me and my team. The client's openness and trust allowed for many great things to happen. The real achievement, for me, was being able to provide the client with something out of this world that was just what he wanted.

Together, we created a home that is a source of warmth and comfort for this family; a place where many pleasant memories will be made for those lucky enough to visit – now and long into the future.

cAsSidaE cOttAGe

There is one place in this world that I cherish with all my heart, and that is Stradbroke Island in Queensland. I've been holidaying there since I was a child and I feel more at home there than anywhere else. Life on the island really does take on its own kind of rhythm. From the minute you drive onto the barge or step onto the water taxi, everything just starts to wind down. All your worries are left on the mainland. It is the place I always go when life turns upside down. Long morning beach walks and swimming in the ocean help to clear my mind and reset my thoughts to a fresh, happy and healthy outlook.

When looking to find a new house on the island, after selling the old cottage I'd owned for sixteen years, I was determined to find a spot that had a wonderful view of the ocean but was close enough to the beach that I could walk down and not have to drive. As I would be living between this house and my place in Melbourne, the property also needed to be manageable and not too big.

As luck would have it, I discovered a tiny, awkward old house just up the hill from my original cottage. Despite its gorgeous views,

Cassidae Cottage had been on the market for quite some time. The building is made up of two hexagonal weatherboard pavilions, and I suspect most people would find it hard to know what to do with a house that shape. But for me, it was perfect. It had everything I wanted and, more importantly, was in dire need of a renovation, which meant I could put my own stamp on it. I quickly worked up a plan that would see me completely renovate the house over six weeks. I enlisted the help of my wonderful builder, Luke Noble, and cabinet-maker, Craig Madders, who worked their magic and got everything completed so that I could move in on schedule.

One of the pavilions contains the living room and kitchen, while the other houses two bedrooms, a bathroom and a powder room. All of the original windows were quite small and framed in brown aluminium. I replaced them with large floor-to-ceiling timber windows and sliding doors, which has added so much light, increased the view of the ocean from inside, and makes the house feel much more open. Removing the 1990s cornices and square setting from the ceilings made everything feel modern and fresh.

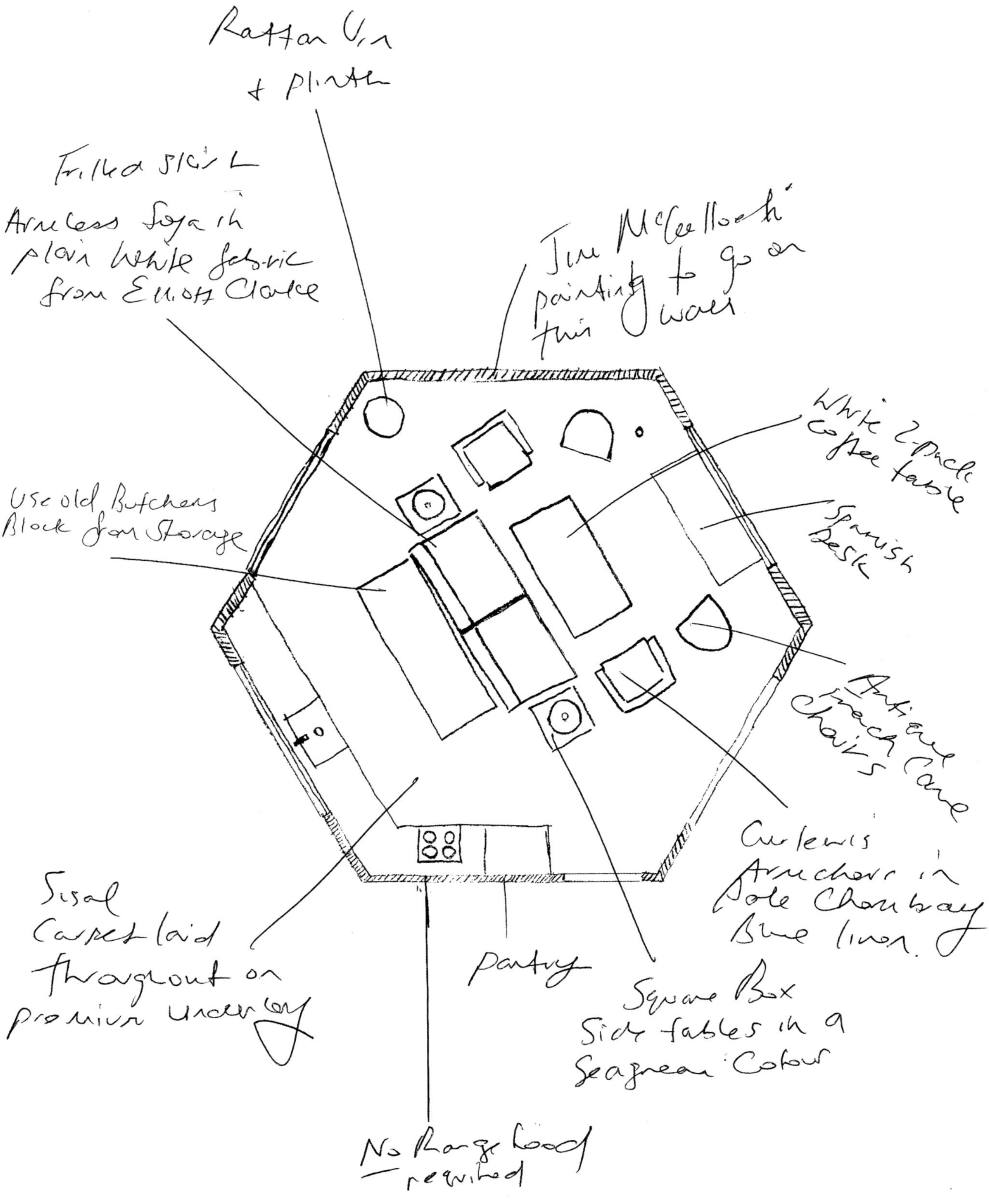

Rattan Urn
& plinth

Frilled Skirt
Armless Sofa in
plain White fabric
from Elliott Clarke

Jim McCulloch
painting to go on
this wall

White 2 pack
coffee table

Spanish
Desk

Use old Butchers
Block for Storage

Antique
French Cane
Chairs

Cu Lewis
Armchairs in
Pale Chambray
Blue Linen.

Sisal
Carpet laid
throughout on
premium underlay

Square Box
Side tables in a
Seagreen Colour

Pantry

No Range hood
required

223

The existing blue-and-white-laminate kitchen was very dated, and jutted awkwardly into the living room, leaving no space for a comfortable living area. To solve the problem, I decided to create a dual-purpose kitchen–living room. I aligned the new kitchen so that it runs along the lengths of two sides of the hexagonal structure, and added an old butcher's block that acts as both a central bench and a sofa table. The sofa backs directly onto the butcher's block and thus sits centrally in the hexagon, providing anyone sitting there with a view directly out the window to the ocean. I arranged a number of mismatched armchairs in the room for conversational seating. The multifunctional design of the new kitchen–living area makes far better use of the space and in turn makes the room feel larger and more comfortable.

When it came to furniture, I knew I wanted to do something a little bit simpler, something more restrained and less patterned, than I normally would. This house needed to be restful, peaceful; somewhere I could take a breath, away from all the patterns and colours with which I usually surround myself. As my sons were a bit older, I felt it was the right time to allow myself the luxury of an all-white sofa. So that it didn't feel bulky in the room, I decided to make it an armless sofa with a frilled skirt. I picked two blue and white patterns for the scatter cushions, and plain soft-pink and pale-blue linen for the armchairs. The bright sea-green box side tables that bookend the sofa reference a large abstract painting by Melbourne artist Jim McCullough, which hangs in the same room and provides a wonderful, fun and unexpected jab of colour.

Unfortunately, there were no timber floors under the original vinyl, so to save money and make the house feel cosier, I installed sisal carpeting throughout. Its light, natural colouring has made the house feel a lot bigger, and it's actually much easier to keep clean than floorboards – timber floors at the beach always feel like they are sandy, no matter how often you vacuum!

As always, at Cassidae Cottage I have indulged my love of mixing antique and new pieces. For example, in the living room I paired an antique Spanish desk (which I work at, but which also hosts collections of beloved things) with a simple white coffee table and geometric, sculptural lamps. I found a lovely cane plinth and urn via Instagram, and love the height it adds to the space. I enjoy filling the urn with local foliage, such as banksia and gum leaves – it is an ever-changing arrangement in the room and draws the eye up to the interestingly shaped ceiling. The living room also has a few beautiful paintings that I love, as well as collections of favourite books stacked up on the floor, shells in trays, and glass candle-lit hurricane lamps for mood lighting at night. These elements add a feeling of casualness and comfort to the otherwise minimal decoration I have chosen.

In my bedroom, it is all about the view. Waking up and looking out through those wonderfully large windows to see the ocean directly in front of me, and the bushland just to the right, is absolutely stunning. I feel like I am living in a treehouse. As the room is small, I opted for a timber-frame bed base, so I can slide storage baskets underneath. There is no bed head, as I wanted to hang a painting by Sally Lee Anderson above the bed – it's a large piece and takes up almost the entire wall. Simple white bed linen and a decorative cushion, bed-end throw and soft-pink lamps with grass-woven shades create a lovely, peaceful and comfortable bedroom.

In the guest bedroom I wanted to do something a bit wild, as it is a room with an awkward shape and no view. I covered all the walls in a bold red and white toile wallpaper and painted the window frames, skirting boards and cabinetry in a matching red. I have twin beds in this room, so that my boys can stay here when they are with me, and it can double as a guest room at other times. It's such a fun room; it really wraps you up when you stay in it. It's proof that any room, no matter what shape it is, and even if it appears to have nothing going for it, can look and feel amazing with a bit of creative thought and a confident approach.

The new house on Stradbroke Island is perfect for my needs. It is my home when I am in Brisbane and provides my family with everything we could possibly want for simple living on the island. Some days we go to the beach for a few hours and then return home for lunch and an afternoon rest. Slow walks in the late afternoon at sunset on Home Beach with my boys and Neddie, our golden retriever, feel comforting and familiar to me. I remember doing the same thing with my parents, brothers and our family retriever when I was young. The name of this favourite beach has always resonated with me, as I do feel so at home there – I have been walking this beach for over thirty-five years.

Of an evening, enjoying a simple home-cooked dinner on the deck with family – music playing, candles lit, table set and sea breezes floating in through the trees – there is nowhere else I'd rather be. This is my idea of heaven.

ACKNOWLEDGEMENTS

It really does take a village, and I had an amazing one helping me to create this book.

To Penny Sheehan, my design assistant, who is the most focused, energetic, creative, loyal and hard-working person I have ever had the privilege of working with. From the bottom of my heart, I thank you, dearest Penny, for all those long hours, weekends and nights you spent with me getting everything so perfect. I love working with you!

To my friend, the incredibly talented photographer Tim Salisbury – WOW is pretty much how I would sum it up. I have worked with you since your very early days, and you know just how to capture the magic in my rooms. Thank you, Tim, your work in this book is seriously divine. I hope you don't get too busy for me now!

To Eliza McNamee, who works in my office in Brisbane, your sketches and drawings are incredible. You are always so clever in determining exactly what I want to achieve. I love working with you and I thank you very much for all that you do for me. In fact, to my entire team – Greer, Mel, Kelly, Lisa, Eliza and Penny – thank you for everything. You make it all happen, I absolutely love working with you every day and I just couldn't do it without you.

Over the three months of crazy, intense photo shoots, we were humbled by the generosity of our friends and suppliers. To Hacienda Flowers, Norwood Roses and Bess Paddington – thank you for all the beautiful flowers you supplied to us. Thank you to Jess at Wallrocks Antiques in Brisbane for lending us a few items to fill the odd gap, and for letting us shoot in your very inspiring mecca of antiques. Thank you to Emma Sheehan for the hand-painted page background on the Contents page. And to Tash at Obsidian Hair for all your time doing my hair – often at the very last minute! And, of course, thank you to my dearest friend Sophie Trevethan, for your invaluable help on some of those big shoot days. I am so lucky to have you in my life.

It goes without saying that this book would not be possible without all of my kind and fabulous clients, who trust me to do what I do. These pages show the rooms you all love and live in every day, and that makes me feel very proud. Thank you for allowing us into your homes to photograph the work we did for you. It means the world to me to be able to share the magic we helped you create.

To Kirsten Abbott at Thames & Hudson, for believing in me again and for letting us create a book that is 'outside the box' and so representative of me and my work. I am so grateful to you. Thank you, Kirsten! And to the kind and polite Sam Palfreyman and Jess Redman, for all the edits and support throughout the entire process. Thank you, too, to John at ColourChiefs for helping Penny with the technical side of the book's design. You are always so generous and good to us.

Thank you to my family for your support, critique (because we all need some of that in our lives), love and guidance always.

Thank you to my partner, Luke, for your ceaseless love, encouragement and kindness. You kept pushing me, behind the scenes, to keep going and I am so grateful for everything you do for me.

And finally, thank you to my children, Harry and Max, who understand how crazy things can get. Their enduring and unwavering love is what keeps me going every day. I love you both with all my heart and everything I do is for you. You are my everything.

CREDITS

1

2

3

4

5 6 7

8

9

10

11

12

13

14

15

16

1. Wallpaper: Handpainted 'Island Garden' created by de Gournay in collaboration with Anna Spiro; Scatter cushion in Raoul Textiles Flamestitch col. Olive.

2. (Right) Antique mural panel.

3. (Left) Antique pattern designs. (Right) Splatter texture background by Emma Sheehan.

4. Original artwork by Bronte Leighton-Dore.

5. Wallpaper: Handpainted 'Island Garden' created by de Gournay in collaboration with Anna Spiro; Sofa scatter cushions in Manuel Canovas Villars col. Caraibes; Armchair in Vanderhurd Flower Cut-Out col. Jade/Moonstone; Woven ceramic lamp bases by Matilda Goad with shades in Baker Lifestyle Avila col. Spice.

6. Curtains in Anna Spiro Textiles Otto col. Green; Antique chair in Vanderhurd Perspectivo col. Tobacco/Moonstone; Sofa in Brunschwig & Fils Arbre Fleuri col. Beige; Square cushion in Teyssier Hawkeswood col. Original; central rectangular cushion in Soane Fez col. Red.

7. (Left) Curtains in Blithfield Oakleaves col. Natural Yellow; Square arm sofa in Anna Spiro Textiles Paniola col. Green, Navy and Pale Blue.

8. Artwork above mantle *Number 9* by Emma Sheehan; Blue sofa in Brunschwig & Fils Chancellor Strie II col. Sky; Pink sofa in Anna Spiro Textiles Grandma's Quilt col. Pink; Coote&Co. pineapple lamps with shades in Vanderhurd Flower Cut-Out col. Coral/Champignon.

9. Wallpaper: Nina Campbell Les Rêves Domiers Indigo/Ivory; Roman blinds in Anna Spiro Textiles Camona col. Blue; Shades in Edit Big Spots; Ottoman in No. 9 Thompson Karapinar col. Riviera; Armchair in Cassandra Harper Floral; Bamboo sofa in Anna Spiro Textiles Grandma's Quilt col. Green.

10. (Left) Original artwork by Madeleine Peters. (Right) Background fabric and sofa in GP & J Baker Rockbird Signature col. Indigo; Armchair in Lisa Fine Textiles Kalindi col. Dusty Rose; Artworks from left to right: *Silver Princess* by Adam Pyett, Original artwork by Alessandro Ljubicic, *Everlasting Daisies* by Laura Jones, *Coledale Cottage* by Christopher Zanko, *Forget it* by Monica Rohan.

11. Wallpaper: Handpainted 'Island Garden' created by de Gournay in collaboration with Anna Spiro; Scatter cushion in Manuel Canovas Villars col. Caraibes; Woven ceramic lamp base by Matilda Goad with shade in Baker Lifestyle Avila col. Spice; Anna Spiro Design Tulu Mirror.

12. (Left) Bench in Décors Barbares Sadko col. Pink; Vintage framed prints. (Right) Wallpaper: Ben Pentreath for Morris & Co. Bird & Anemone col. Olive/Turquoise; Artworks from top to bottom: Vintage painting, Original artwork by Jane Guthleben.

13. (Left) Wallpaper: Anna Spiro Textiles Cartouche col. Green; Artworks from top to bottom: Antique cabbage oil painting in original frame, Antique still life painting in original frame. (Right) Background: Antique quilt.

14. Roman blinds in Décors Barbares Dans la Forêt col. Original; Blue armchair in Anna Spiro Textiles Grandma's Quilt col. Blue; Alice sofa in Jennifer Shorto NZO River col. Anthracite; Footstool in Lisa Fine Textiles Kalindi col. Lipstick.

15. (Left) Antique textile. (Right) Handwritten calligraphy by Sam Pauletto.

16. (Left) Ceiling wallpaper: Pierre Frey La Pannonie col. Printemps; Ottoman in Seema Krish Juhu col. Panna Green; Sofa in Thibaut Malibu col. Sky Blue; Armchair in Turnell & Gigon Bannister Hall col. Natural Ground; Scatter cushion in Claire Frost Lydia Ikat; Lampshade in Anna Spiro Textiles Grandma's Quilt col. Blue. Patterns.

17

18

19

20

21

22

23

24

25

26

27

28

29

30

31

32

17. (Left) Pip Spiro wave artwork for Anna Spiro Textiles Islet collaboration. (Right) Armchair in Turnell & Gigon Bannister Hall col. Natural Ground; Scatter cushion in Claire Frost Lydia Ikat.

18. (Left) Original artwork by Bronte Leighton-Dore; Wallpaper: Ben Pentreath for Morris & Co. Bird & Anemone col. Olive/Turquoise. (Right) Curtains in Anna Spiro Textiles Otto col. Green; Antique chair in Vanderhurd Perspectivo col. Tobacco/Moonstone; Sofa in Brunschwig & Fils Arbre Fleuri col. Beige; White armchair scatter cushion in Colefax and Fowler Persis col. Red.

19. (Left) Wallpaper: Handpainted 'Island Garden' created by de Gournay in collaboration with Anna Spiro; Gathered curtains in Anna Spiro Textiles Otto col. Blue. (Right) Wallpaper: Handpainted 'Island Garden' created by de Gournay in collaboration with Anna Spiro; Scatter cushions in Raoul Textiles Flamestitch col. Olive.

20. Wallpaper: Ottoline Improvisation Number 1 – Red; Curtains in Brunschwig & Fils Birds of a Feather Linen col. Celadon; Dining chairs in Anna Spiro Textiles Tattie Tartan.

21. Framed print: *The Jetty at Currigee* by Tim Salisbury; Sofa in Anna Spiro Textiles Grandma's Quilt col. Teal; Armchairs in Anna Spiro Textiles Camona col. Green, Taupe and Turquoise; Lampshade in Peter Dunham Zaya col. Blue/Green; Original artwork by Christopher Jewitt.

22. Armchairs in Manuel Canovas Floral.

23. Both background patterns by Anna Spiro for Anthropologie collaboration.

24. (Left) Anna Spiro Design office sketch by Eliza McNamee. (Right) Wallpaper: Handpainted 'Island Garden' created by de Gournay in collaboration with Anna Spiro; Sofa scatter cushions in Manuel Canovas Villars col. Caraibes; Armchair in Vanderhurd Flower Cut-Out col. Jade/Moonstone; Ceramic lamp bases by Matilda Goad with shades in Baker Lifestyle Avila col. Woven Spice.

25. (Right) Bedhead in Décors Barbares Natacha col. Beige; Bed cushion in Soane Fez Stripe col. Red; Lampshade in Décors Barbares Aurel col. Original.

26. (Left) Armchair in Annie Coop Morton; Scatter cushion in Ottoline Chintamani col. Antique Green; Artworks from left to right: *Forget it* by Monica Rohan, *Two women talking story by the fire* by Sally M Nangala Mulda, *Those Shoes* by Laura Jones, *Day is Done* by Michael Muir; Vases on chest: *Oxidised Technicolour part 2* by Jason Fitzgerald, *Bird* by Dulcie Sharp. (Right) Artworks from left to right: *Silver Princess* by Adam Pyett, *Everlasting Daisies* by Laura Jones, *Coledale Cottage* by Christopher Zanko.

27. Furniture upholstery and cushions made from client's personal collection of vintage fabric pieces; Lampshades by Sachs & Cornish.

28. Brunschwig & Fils Digby Tent Linen and Cotton Print col. Moroccan Blue.

29. Armchairs in Anna Spiro Textiles Cartouche col. Blue; Sofa in Anna Spiro Textiles Camona col. Blue; Sofa scatter cushions in Kettlewell Collection Aiko col. Indigo.

30. Ottoman in Seema Krish Juhu col. Panna Green; Armchair in Turnell & Gigon Bannister Hall col. Natural Ground; Scatter cushion in Claire Frost Lydia Ikat.

31. Wallpaper: Pierre Frey Braquenié La Comedie col. Bleu.

32. Left sofa in Nicole Fabre Designs Vaison col. Bleu Anglais; Lampshades in Vanderhurd Flower Cut-Out col. Jade/Moonstone; Armchair in GP & J Baker Bamboo Bird col. Aqua/Teal; Ottoman in Elliott Clarke Queensbury Stripe col. Aqua; Yellow sofa in Marvic Renishaw col. Mimosa; Scatter cushions in Nine Muses Greek Plate.

CREDITS

33

34

35

36

37

38

39

40

41

43

44

42

45

47

48

46

33. *Moths 16* by Allyson Reynolds; Central sofa in Nicole Fabre Designs Vaison col. Bleu Anglais; Left sofa in Colefax and Fowler Eaton Check col. Sage; Armchair in GP & J Baker Bamboo Bird col. Aqua/Teal; Lampshades in Vanderhurd Flower Cut-Out col. Jade/Moonstone.

34. Furniture floor plan sketch by Eliza McNamee.

35. Original artwork by Paul Ryan; Armchair in Olinda col. Yellow; Sofa in Guy Goodfellow Fez Weave col. Persimmon; Antique footstool in Décors Barbares Naboika col. Indigo; Curtains in Ralph Lauren Antibes Batik col. Chambray.

36. From left to right: Ralph Lauren Antibes Batik col. Chambray, Thibaut Glennifer col. Navy and Red, Olinda col. Yellow, Décors Barbares Naboika col. Indigo, Redelman Standish Vert, Décors Barbares Sadko col. Blue, Ralph Lauren Chiangmai Silk col. Indigo, Guell Lamadrid Steve Stripe.

37. Wallpaper: Pierre Frey Braquenié La Comedie col. Bleu; Roman blinds in Anna Spiro Textiles Nihi col. Shell with Vintage Decorative Trim.

38. (Left) Clockwise from top left: Armchair in Cassandra Harper Floral with Cushion in Ash Block Printing Auroa col. Marigold, Curtains in Blithfield Oakleaves col. Natural Yellow, Bedhead in Schumacher Madura Floral Stitchery col. Indigo and Ivory, Wallpaper: Anna Spiro Textiles Cartouche col. Blue, Alice sofa in Lewis & Wood Chelsea Check col. Corn, Cushion in Lisa Fine Textiles Kalindi col. Saffron. (Right) Left to right: Antique artwork in original frame, Window curtains in Anna Spiro Textiles Otto col. Blue, Wallpaper: Handpainted 'Island Garden' created by de Gournay in collaboration with Anna Spiro.

39. *Suburban Landscape* by Amalia Keefer.

40. (Left) Client's own antique artworks, (Right) Background: Anna Spiro pattern for Anthropologie collaboration.

41. (Left) Illustrations by Eliza McNamee and Penny Sheehan. (Right) Square scatter cushion in Décors Barbares Casse-noisette col. Pink; Central cushion in Anna Spiro Textiles Marigold Inverted col. Brown; Lampshade in Bernard Thorp Pineapple Leaf on Oskar Natural Linen col. Wild Ecru Pink.

42. Blue sofa in Brunschwig & Fils Chancellor Strie II in Sky; Pink sofa in Anna Spiro Textiles Grandma's Quilt col. Pink; Scatter cushions in Anna Spiro Textiles Marigold Solid col. Yellow; Coote&Co. pineapple lamps with shades in Vanderhurd Flower Cut-Out col. Coral/Champignon; Curlewis armchairs in JAB Switch Stripe col. Green.

43. Curtains in Décors Barbares Natacha col. Blue; Top left yellow still life by Stewart Free; Lower right floral still life by Stewart Free; Collection of client's personal vintage pieces.

44. Camp Hill sitting room sketch by Eliza McNamee.

45. Curtains in Blithfield Oakleaves col. Natural Yellow; Sofa in Anna Spiro Textiles Paniola col. Green, Navy and Pale Blue; Armchair in GP & J Baker Bamboo Bird col. Aqua/Teal.

46. Wallpaper: Thibaut Textured Wallpaper; Sofa in antique Redelman's fabric (now discontinued); Curtains and Roman blinds in Anna Spiro Textiles Kahuna Solid col. Pale Blue; Cane armchair in Vanderhurd Flower Cut-Out col. Jade/Moonstone.

47. Scatter cushions left to right: Anna Spiro Textiles Grandma's Quilt col. Green, Blue indigo antique cushion, Anna Spiro Textiles Marigold Solid col. Taupe.

48. (Left) *Le Couple, Sicily* by Akila Berjaoui; Sculpture by Ari Athans; Wallpaper: Phillip Jeffries Juicy Jute Grasscloth; Alice sofa in Marvic Renishaw col. Chambray; Dining chair in Vanderhurd Perspectivo 1009-5 col. Azul/Moonstone. (Right) Illustrations by Eliza McNamee and Penny Sheehan.

49

50

51

52

53

54

55

56

57

58

59

60

61

62

63

64

49. *She Raw #29* by Lilli Waters; Matilda Goad lamp base with Matilda Goad Signature Scallop Lampshade in Raffia with Cream Trim; Antique bed in Vanderhurd Cordoba col. Seaglass/ Moonstone; Bed cushion in Anna Spiro Textiles Cartouche col. Navy Blue.

50. (Left) *Blue Laps* by Aquabumps. (Right) Illustrations by Eliza McNamee and Penny Sheehan.

51. Wallpaper: Anna Spiro Textiles Cartouche col. Teal; Curtains in Anna Spiro Textiles Marigold Solid col. Taupe; Bedhead and armchair cushion in Travers Beaumont Indienne; Bed cushions in Claire Frost Lydia Ikat.

52. Wallpaper: Soane Scrolling Fern Silhouette col. Cream on Jasper Blue; Bedheads in Blithefield Ikat Check col. Dusty Blue; Lampshade in Colefax and Fowler Seafern col. Blue.

53. (Left) Illustrations by Eliza McNamee and Penny Sheehan. (Right) Wallpaper: Thibaut Sherrill Paisley col. Blue; Barstools in Thibaut Sherill Paisley col. Blue.

54. (Left) Wallpaper: Ottoline Improvisation Number 1 – Red; Cabinet curtains in Anna Spiro Textiles Grandma's Quilt col. Pink; Lampshades in Décors Barbares Aurel col. Original. (Right) Original artworks by Caitlin McGauley.

55. Wallpaper: Pierre Frey Braquenié La Comedie col. Bleu; Roman blinds in Anna Spiro Textiles Nihi col. Shell with vintage decorative trim.

56. (Left) Illustrations by Eliza McNamee and Penny Sheehan. (Right) Wallpaper: Pierre Frey Braquenié La Comedie col. Bleu; Anna Spiro Design Tulu Mirror.

57. Wallpaper: Schumacher Bakara Leaf col. Delft.

58. (Left) Curtains in Décors Barbares Ete Moscovite col. Original. (Right) Curtains in Michael S Smith Jasper Meleaya col. Indigo.

59. (Right) Original artwork by Nicholas Harding.

60. (Left) Roman blinds in Décors Barbares Casse-noisette col. Bleu; Framed botanical prints by Lucy Augé. (Right) Illustrations by Eliza McNamee and Penny Sheehan.

61. (Left) Artworks from left to right: *Moths* by Allyson Reynolds, *Landscape* by Marina Strocchi, Framed botanical prints by Lucy Augé. (Right) *Water Dance* by Gina Fishman; Lampshades in Soane Persian Flower Lapis.

62. (Left) Illustrations by Eliza McNamee and Penny Sheehan. (Right) Gathered curtains in Colefax and Fowler Appledore Check.

63. Original artwork by Bronte Leighton-Dore; Rug Establishment 'Leaf Rug; Antique armchairs in Pierre Frey Naomie col. Paon.

64. *Lukes Lane North, 2019* by Guy Maestri.

CREDITS

66

67

68

69

70

71

72

73

74

75

76

77

78

79

81

80

66. Curtains in Michael S Smith Jasper Remy col. Blue; Armchair in Nicole Fabre Designs Latour col. Cactus; Sofa scatter cushions in Colefax and Fowler Persis col. Aqua; Rug Establishment 'Leaf Rug.

67. (Left) Original artwork by Bronte Leighton-Dore; Side chair in Nicholas Herbert Donatello col. Indigo/Cream. (Right) Bragg & Co. Ginger Jar Lamp col. Caramel; Bragg & Co. raffia console.

68. Curtains in Michael S Smith Jasper Remy col. Blue; Antique armchairs in Pierre Frey Naomie col. Paon; Alice sofa in Lewis & Wood Chelsea Check col. Corn; Cushion in Lisa Fine Textiles Kalindi col. Saffron; Rug Establishment 'Leaf Rug.

69. Curtains in Michael S Smith Jasper Remy col. Blue; Curlewis armchairs in Nicole Fabre Designs Latour col. Cactus; Scatter cushions in Jennifer Shorto Petrol col. Blue.

70. (Right) Antique print; Armchair in Michael S Smith Templeton Landera col. Tan; Desk chair in Penny Morrison Zig Zag Stripe col. Azure/Kingfisher; Desk lampshade in Rose Tarlow Chablish col. Bay Blue/Haze.

71. Original artwork by Sally Anderson; Sofa in Gaston y Daniela Semilla; Sofa central scatter cushions in Mulberry Home Walton col. Indigo; Sofa outer scatter cushions in Flora Soames Cornucopia col. Ruby/Sage; Armchairs in Michael S Smith Templeton Landera col. Tan; Lampshades in Lisa Fine Luxor col.Coco/Natural.

72. Wallpaper: Kravet Natural Grassweave; Curtains in Turnell & Gigon Nicky Haslam Seafern col. Snowdrop; Sofa in Marvic Toile Carreaux col. Natural; Bed cushions in Rose Tarlow Florentina col. Taupe/Mushroom; Rug Establishment 'Art Deco Border' Rug.

73. (Left) Roman blinds in Seema Krish Broadway col. Liberty Blue; Bedhead and bed valance in Soane Old Flax col. Bayleaf; Desk chair and bed cushion in Feromie Poulton Stripe. (Right) Original photograph by Tim Salisbury.

74. Central sofa in Elliott Clarke Rocco col. Forest; Left sofa in Gaston y Daniela Semilla col. Agua; Ottoman in Lewis & Wood Palmyra col. Terrafirma; Cane armchairs in Guell Lamadrid Steve Stripe; Scatter cushions in Carolina Irving Patmos Stripe col. Parsley; Lampshades in Lisa Fine Jaisalmer col. Tobacco on Ivory.

75. Sofa and armchair in vintage Rose Tarlow Stripe; Ottoman in Fermoie Wicker; Rectangular scatter cushion in Ralph Lauren Keighley Plaid col. Shetland; Square scatter cushions in Michael S Smith Jasper Malmaison col. Jardin.

76. (Left) Gathered wardrobe curtains in Soane Qajar Stripe col. Original; Antique armchair in Schumacher Gainsborough Velvet col. Delft; Scatter cushion in Décors Barbares Dans la Foret col. Original; Sofa in Colefax and Fowler Lanard Plaid col. Red.

77. Wing chair in Schumacher Claremont Crewel Embroidery col. Delft; Curtains in Redelman Life Story Linen; Scatter cushion in Redelman Eton col. Gold with decorative braid; Floor lamp shade in Peter Fasano Laundered Linen col. Ocean.

78. Lampshades in Payhembury Marbled Paper.

79. (Left) Original artwork by Paul Ryan; Armchair in Olinda col. Yellow; Sofa in Guy Goodfellow Fez Weave col. Persimmon; Antique footstool in Décors Barbares Naboika col. Indigo; Curtains in Ralph Lauren Antibes Batik col. Chambray; Box-pleated lampshade in Ralph Lauren Chiangmai Silk col. Indigo. (Right) Sofa in Guy Goodfellow Fez Weave col. Persimmon with natural rope piping; Scatter cushion in Guell Lamadrid Steve Stripe.